FUTEBOL
URBAN EUPHORIA IN BRAZIL

PHOTOGRAPHS BY
LEONARDO FINOTTI
AND ED VIGGIANI

LARS MÜLLER
PUBLISHERS

Many nations identify with one sport in particular. But nowhere does the national sport leave a stronger mark on the urban setting than does soccer in Brazil.

In every corner of the city, the chockablock dwellings, no matter how densely packed, give way to rectangular gaps where the Brazilian soul can vent its passion for the sport. An urban pattern is created as if by collective agreement.

From the air and at eye level, the photographers steer our gaze onto the cosmos of a national identity. We can only marvel. But do we really understand?

Lars Müller

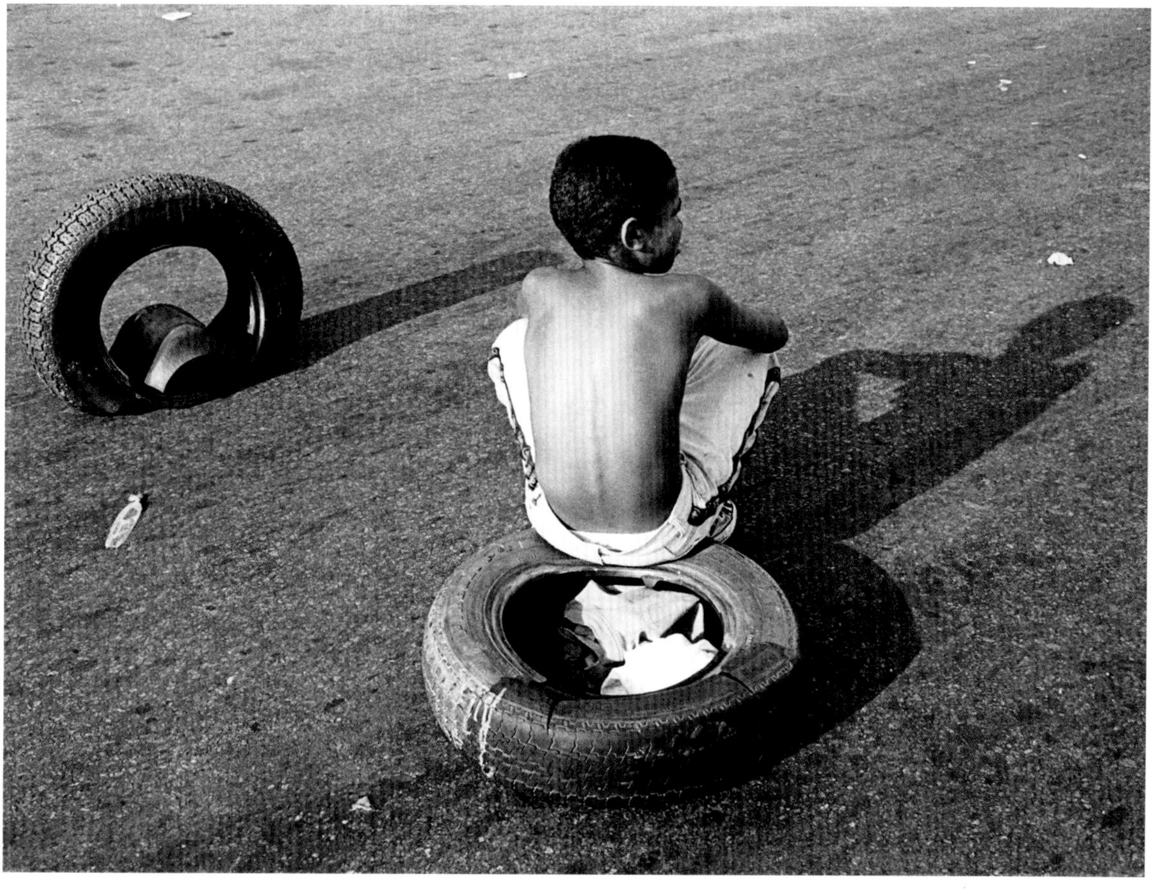

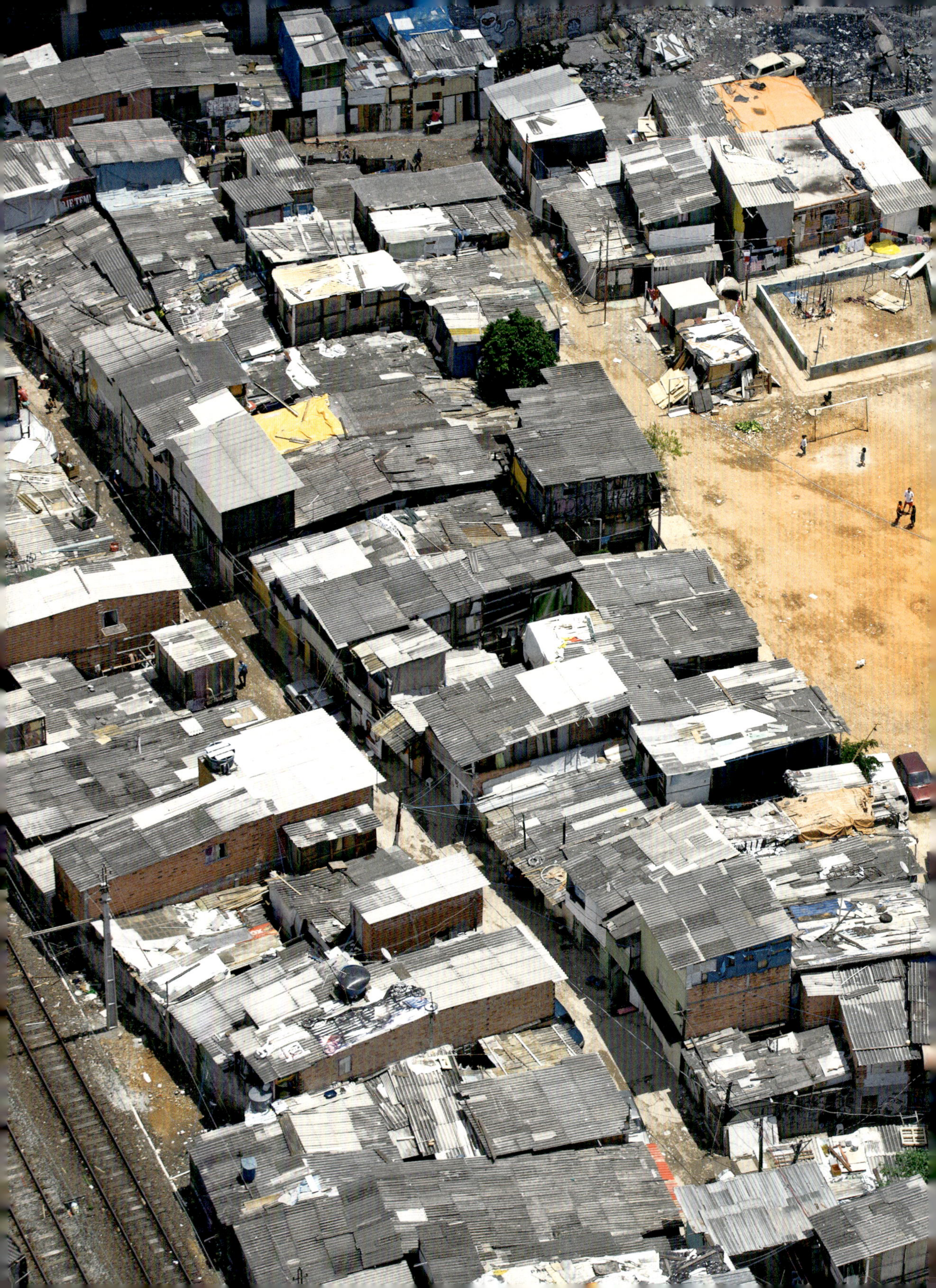

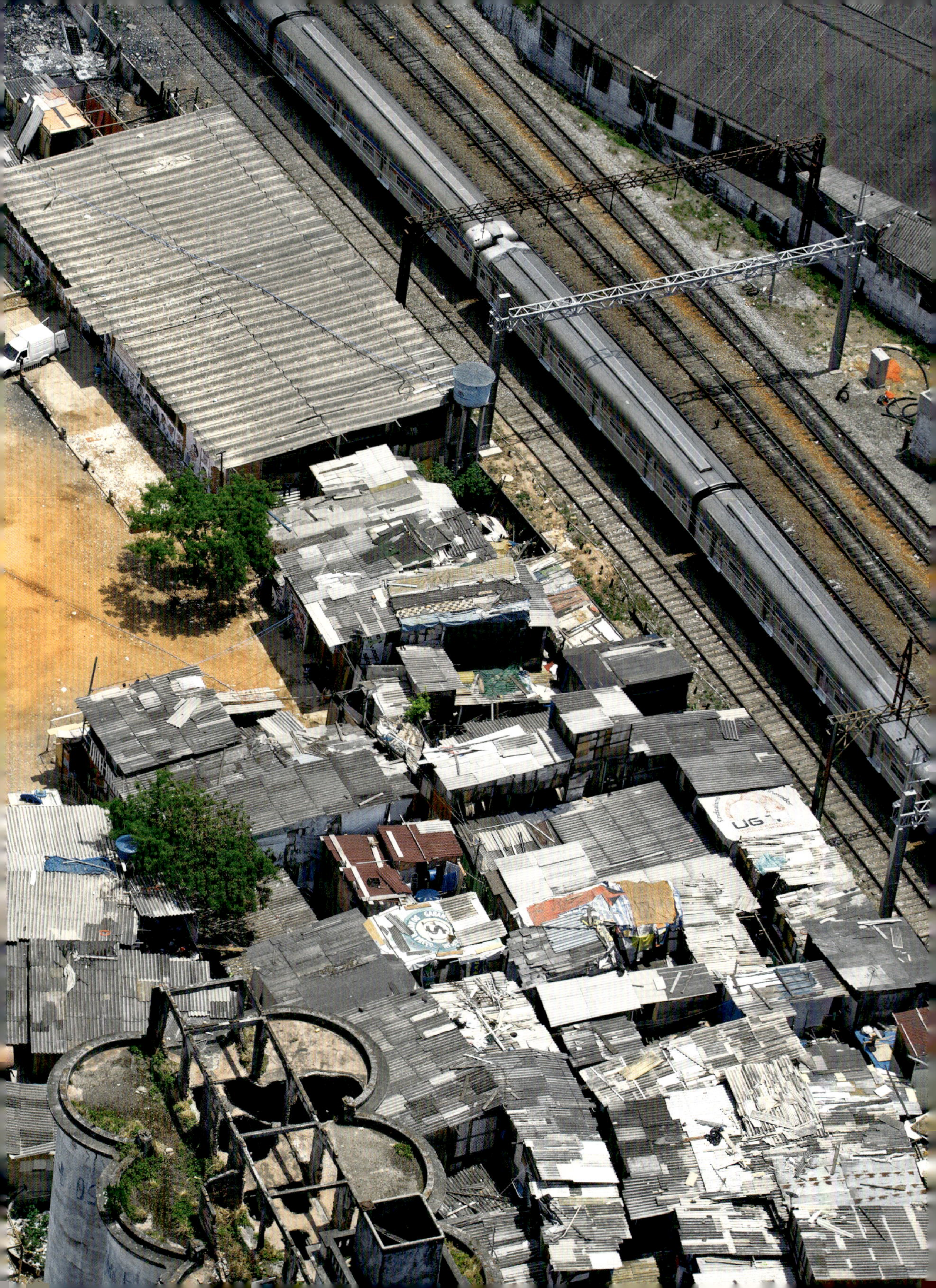

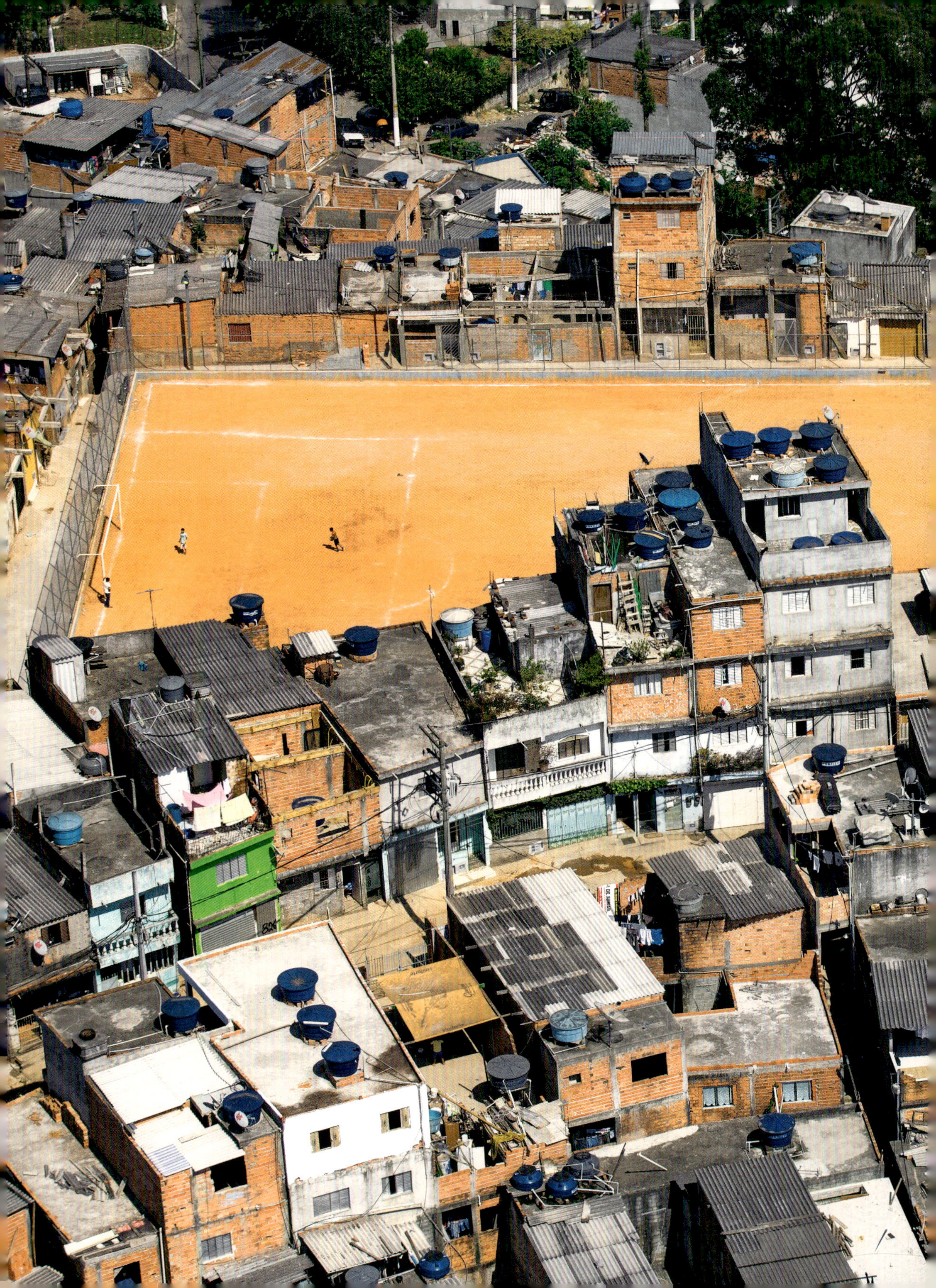

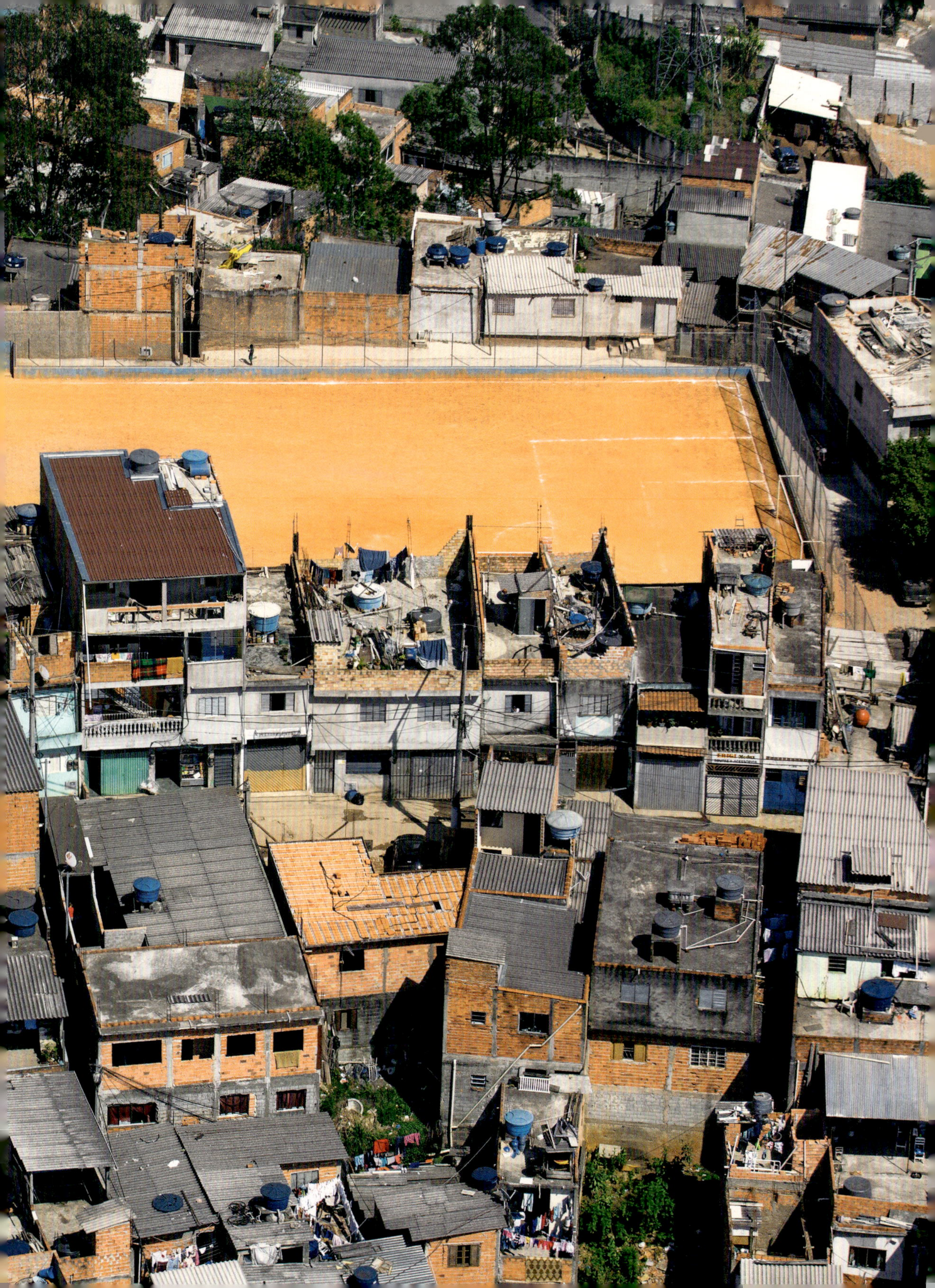

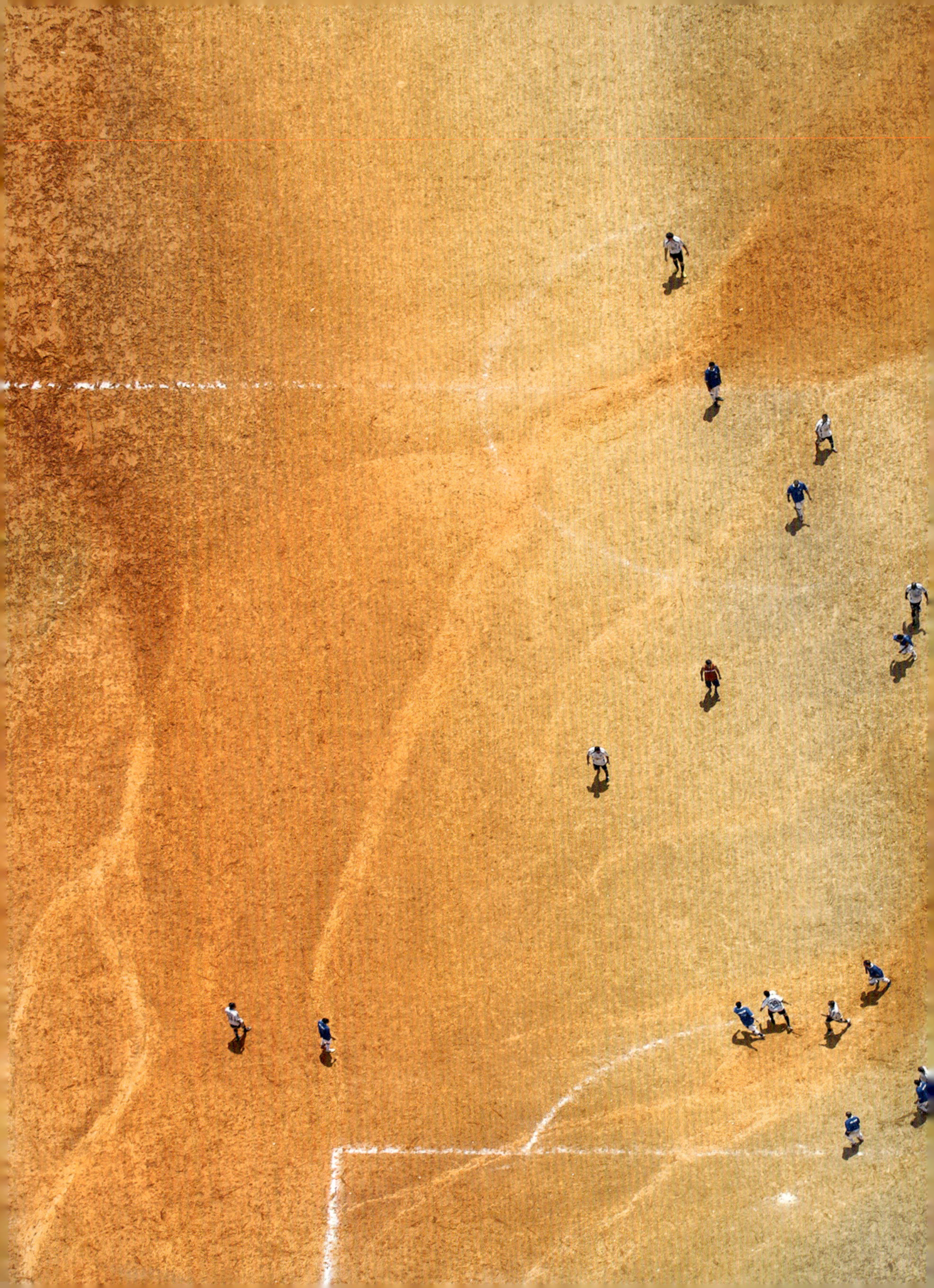

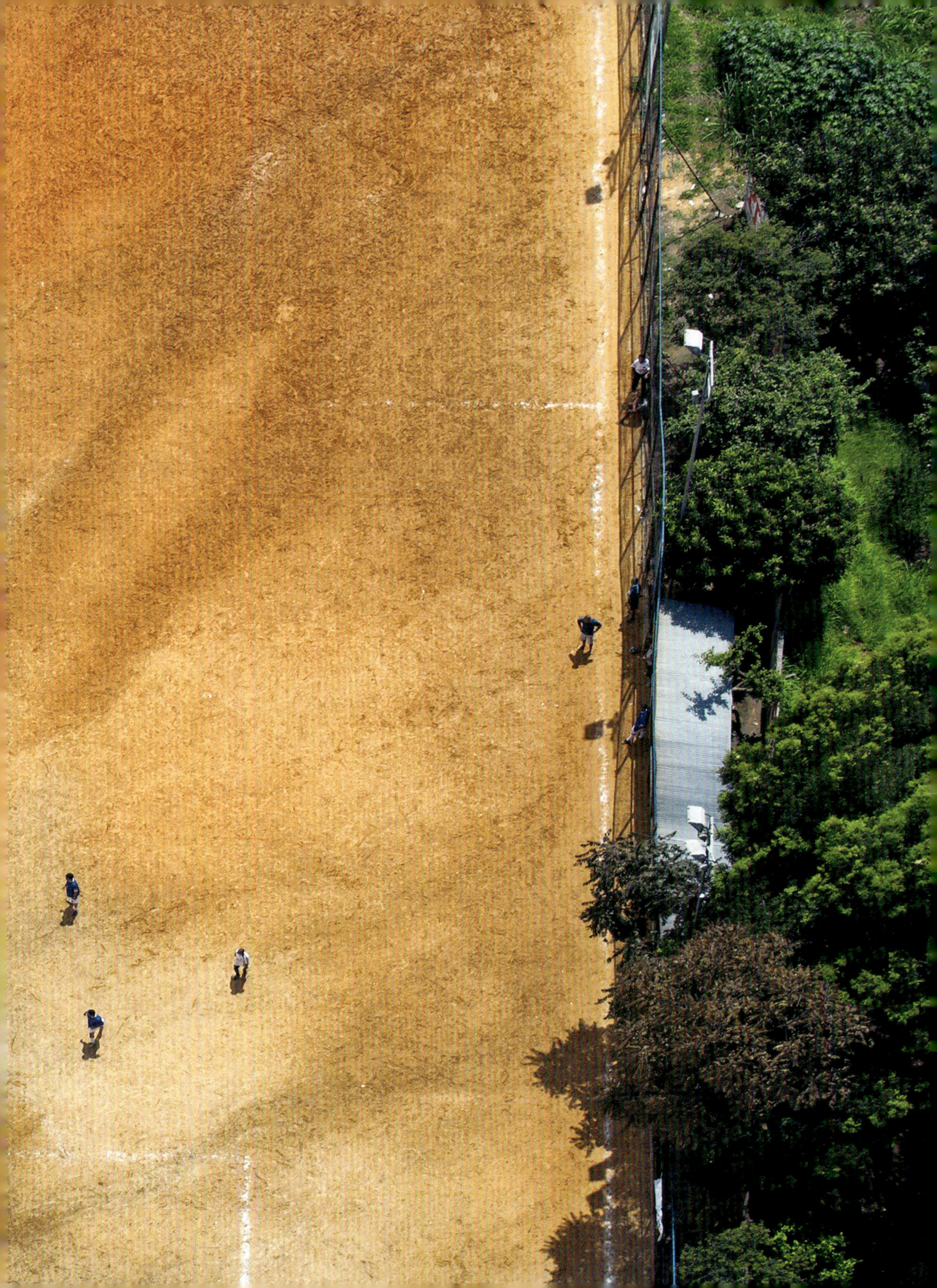

THE BALL, THE MAN, THE GAME WITH THE BALL

Most of all, it's about the fascination of the man for the ball, the sphere he inhabits from the time he's conceived, curled in his mother's round womb, from whence he emerges to play until he dies. It's about losing and winning in the game of life, becoming a star.

They say the Earth is flat. This is another proof of the ball's power, a ball controlled by God, who loves it.

After the first throw-ins and kicks, you contest the ball with an opponent, who is almost always a brother. You start to play, it's your nature. Two against two, eleven against eleven, city against city, country against country, the World Cup. This is the way it is on the entire surface of our blue planet; every four years we are all challenged in a cosmic championship.

A boy alone? Never. A ball made of grass, paper, nylon, rubber (those are the best). Any day now the ball of the "official" games will also have the property of deflating and returning to its original form. I pity the Ronaldos and Neymars who can't play with pebbles, bottle caps, coconuts or fruits of all kinds.

You play in all kinds of spaces and on every kind of surface, each pitch a respected, sacred ground. Some are marked and cleared by little street boys on the periphery of the monumental stadiums that shelter, in miraculous communion, the manifestation of man's highest aspirations, Humanity in harmony.

Radiant sun, terrible cold, nothing better than to play in the rain, the possibilities multiply.

You play while riding elephants, on camels in the desert sands, on polar ice floes; you play barefoot with your toes calloused by the hard ground or dry cement and even wearing computer-designed soccer shoes.

Wherever there's a man, there's a team; on the street, on a corner, in the barracks, the bank, the hospital, the farm, the prison; even if during this incessant search the desire to become Brothers is lost.

Your heart's team is your undying passion, in all its forms, colors, songs, dances, fireworks, flags. No one can say anything against it or they'll end up in the worst fight of their lives.

You play naked in the jungle, all you have to do is paint your body with your preferred colors, barefoot, in caps, berets, hats (just not a top hats) in a cassock, a burka, in all the corners of this giant globe, spinning endlessly, a bending pass delivered by the feet of celestial angels.

The best thing about Sport, not just soccer and other ball games, is its capacity to exercise all the qualities of the players, from their most primitive instincts to the greatest subtleties and refinements of creative ability and civility of the Soul.

The cheers of the fans at the peak of their excitement, as they release their deepest feelings, are the most authentic expression of human connection. The social function of the Sport is its best quality.

The best match happens in the silence of the deepest sleep, in the most colorful and brilliant dream, when you confuse the silky softness of the one you love with the light of the most beautiful pitch.

Free from all responsibilities, conventions, suits and ties and other uniforms, to be able to scream at the top of your lungs the most genuine emotion of the human spirit, which is gooooooaaaal!!!!

Afonso Celso Gárcia Reis

FROM THE COUNTRY TO THE CITY

The impromptu match, the *pelada,* is the paradigm of South American soccer... it's played by barefoot street kids in the middle of the road, on hillsides, on the railroad line, in the bus, in the mangroves, on soft sand, on any unstable surface. In sum, the informal match is a kind of soccer that you play in spite of the ground you play on. In this sport without a field all lines are imaginary—or fluctuating, like the water line on beach soccer, and the goal itself is an abstract thing. What matters is the ball and the boy, the boy and the ball...

—Chico Buarque, "The Boy and the Ball," *O Globo,* June 21, 1998

Barefoot and shirtless, the boy runs after the ball that slips away, escaping his calls. With effort he reaches it and matches his speed to the ball's. Moving together in the direction of the goal, they become a single body. Dominating the ball means to tuck it into the body, to guard it with your foot the way you carry a weapon in your hand, feeling the possession and power to kick the goal shot or the pass, to integrate it into another body, the collective body called the team, bodies in coordinated movement, extensions of the body-head, the thinking body, taking possession of empty spaces, like in a ballet, a dance, or an architectural space. Today is game day. But it's just a street match. The public space is the field on game day.

The field is what's left. The preserved empty space, in fact. A sacred place, nobody dares to occupy it out of respect for really important events. The informal match, the *pelada,* the battle, the stage. Life that is worth living. Would this be the first definition of public space in Brazil?

Seen from the sky, the soccer field is the medieval square that draws in city dwellers; it dates back to the time of Camillo Sitte, an 19th-century architect, painter and city planning theoretician. An empty quadrangle in the tortuous outlines of the dense slum suggests lessons in urban planning and a mastery of scale. The official dimensions of a football field, curiously, vary from 120 to 90 meters long and 90 to 75 meters wide. The Piazza del Campo, in Sienna, Italy, has dimensions praised by the Danish urban planner Jan Gehl, who favors the maximum distance of 100 meters because these dimensions enhance the visual field, circumscribing a space of urban experience and allowing the integration or participation in the events that take place there. If soccer were to inform the design of a park, its lessons would confirm the assessment of the Danish architect and urban planner. The variable measurements of the fields, as well as the proportions between width and length—between 3:4 to 5:6—suggest that soccer has much to offer to the urban planner. First is the principle of adapting space to the tactics of the game.

Soccer molds itself into the available space. It fits into the existing dimensions. The common wisdom of the street match allows the number of players to increase or decrease according to the dimensions of the playing field, with precious awareness of population density. And depending on the proportions of the field, if it is square or more pronouncedly rectangular, the speed of connection between attack and defense varies, and consequently, so do the strategies to create and involve the other in the infinitely more simple task of impeding his progress to an objective (perfection is an objective, defended by the goalie...).[1] The square announces an offensive game, while the rectangle facilitates unassailable defenses.

And even though there is not absolute symmetry between the two sides of the field, or orthogonality between the delimiting lines, or even between the verticality of the erect, standing player and the plane of the field (the playing field of any impromptu game is lightly inclined, and if the visiting team hasn't noticed, the ball is the first to tell them), the sense of fair play is expressed in the careful task of dividing it in half so that in the second half of the game, the sides will be switched between the competing teams, once again shuffling the cards.

The allegorical geometry of the field is so entrenched in the practice of the game that it makes little difference for the *pelada* if the lines are drawn or not on the field. Even if they are invisible, they give weight and measure to the special signifiers: the basic line that divides the field into two halves, one for the attack and one for the defense, one side for my territory and one for my opponent's; the line has the power to invert the behavior of the daring attacker into the most warrior-like defender, zealous in guarding the integrity of his turf. The central circle signals that all directions are possible for the starting point to draw a line. The semicircles and rectangles announce the danger zones and intensify the tension of the game and the acceleration of movements. The lines drawn or imagined on the horizontal plane of the field remind us that the world is representation. And life is the game.

The empty spaces of river flood planes contained in cities have for a long time been a place for

practicing soccer in Brazil. The flood plane fields or flood plane soccer appeared, not always in lowlands or swamps, but always in empty or derelict spaces. The spontaneous practice of soccer on these fields spread out through the cities. They gave rise to a natural or almost spontaneous organization of competition between teams that led to the development of amateur soccer, soccer played with love and without money, joining players and fans who identified with their respective fields, places, myths and rituals in their free time on weekends. Samba schools and social clubs formed the same way, solidifying a culture of place, the sense of belonging to a neighborhood or community that allowed itself to be represented by a team and its stories of glory and memorable failures.

But the flood plane field, in addition to serving those moments of epic battles, was also available for the casual *pelada,* where a team with jerseys challenges one without jerseys. And here the *pelada* teaches us that the game can be played without a whistle or a referee. It represents the anarchical ideal of spontaneous conflict.

For a soccer player, the passage from being an amateur to becoming a professional is like emigrating to another country. There are many stories of Brazilian soccer whizz or idol who, in his spare time, in a surreptitious manner, escape the vigilance imposed by his club to knock the ball around in a *pelada* on a field of beaten earth, to play soccer for fun, to find the country left behind and to remind himself of who he is. What does that flood plane protect? Does that empty space perhaps want to tell us that another city is possible?

The field is what was preserved. Come see the city from the center of the field. Take advantage of the distance and unexpected perspective to withdraw from the day-to-day and to allow the extraordinary into your life. The empty space is an invitation to the match. And the ball, as the poet Paulo Mendes Campos says, is man's essential toy. The ball skims along the ground. The boy kicks the ball, returns it to his companion and receives it further on. In his head the fans are screaming. He kicks. The ball flies. He soars off the ground and fulfills his dream of flying. It's time to run to embrace the team. But he flubbed it.

BETWEEN TWO PERSPECTIVES

The bird's eye view of Leonardo Finotti unveils the nobility of the fields and spaces of soccer in the periphery of big Brazilian cities and examines their relationship to the city. More than a perspective offered by this noteworthy body of photography, what stands out in the reading of these images is a feeling under construction, a meaning in movement that is particular to capturing the dynamics of relationships. The relationship between "field-stage" and "audience-city" in the world theater, the relationships of public and private spaces, between the right to the city and the form that it takes, relationships between culture and urban spaces—all giving a sense of history in the making—are narrated from the most emblematic and representative space of the Brazilian popular imagination: soccer. The presence of these empty spaces gives rise to a new history.

With Ed Viggiani, we are taken to witness and recognize that the practice of soccer is the conquest, invention and subversion of urban space. The city caught unawares and surprised in its moments of leisure, offers openings where bodies come together and synchronize in the movement of the ball. Soccer asks very little to accomplish the inspiring transformation and affirmation of life in city spaces.

In the works of Finotti and Viggiani, there is a significant difference of distances or proximities between registers and points of reference. From watching from a distance to sharing the experience of playing or being a fan, in the middle of the action, we traverse a dissonant narrative, where we learn that the cracks, the pauses, the empty spaces between things preserve the promise of poetry and the dribble in the city of the future, in the destiny of things, in the determinism of life and luck of the game.

Soccer invites the city to learn how to treat its empty spaces—like the boy who sits on a tire, anxiously waiting for his turn to enter the game.

Luís Antônio Jorge

1 Verse of the song "Meio de Campo", by Gilberto Gil, on the album *Cidade do Salvador,* 1974.

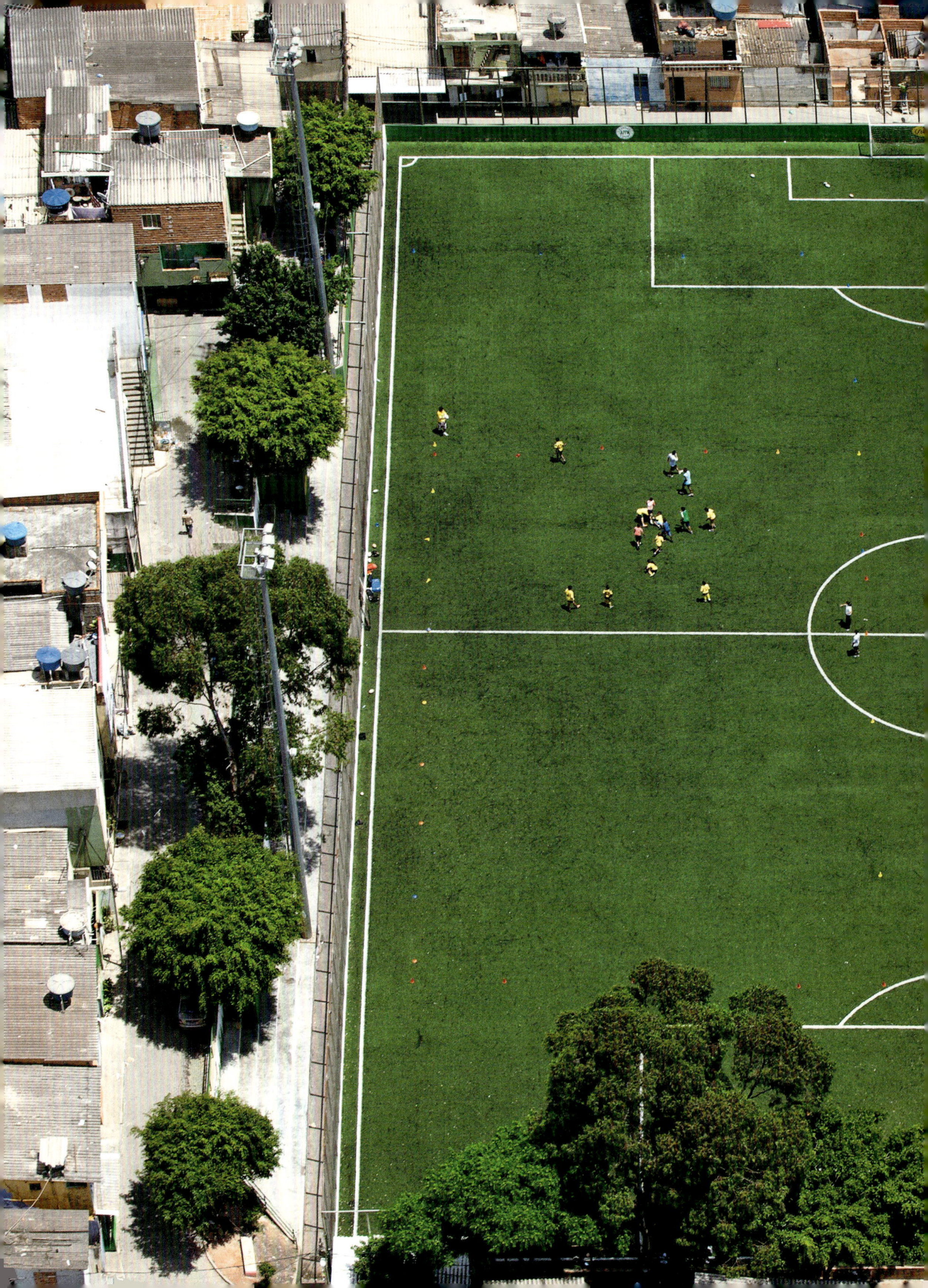

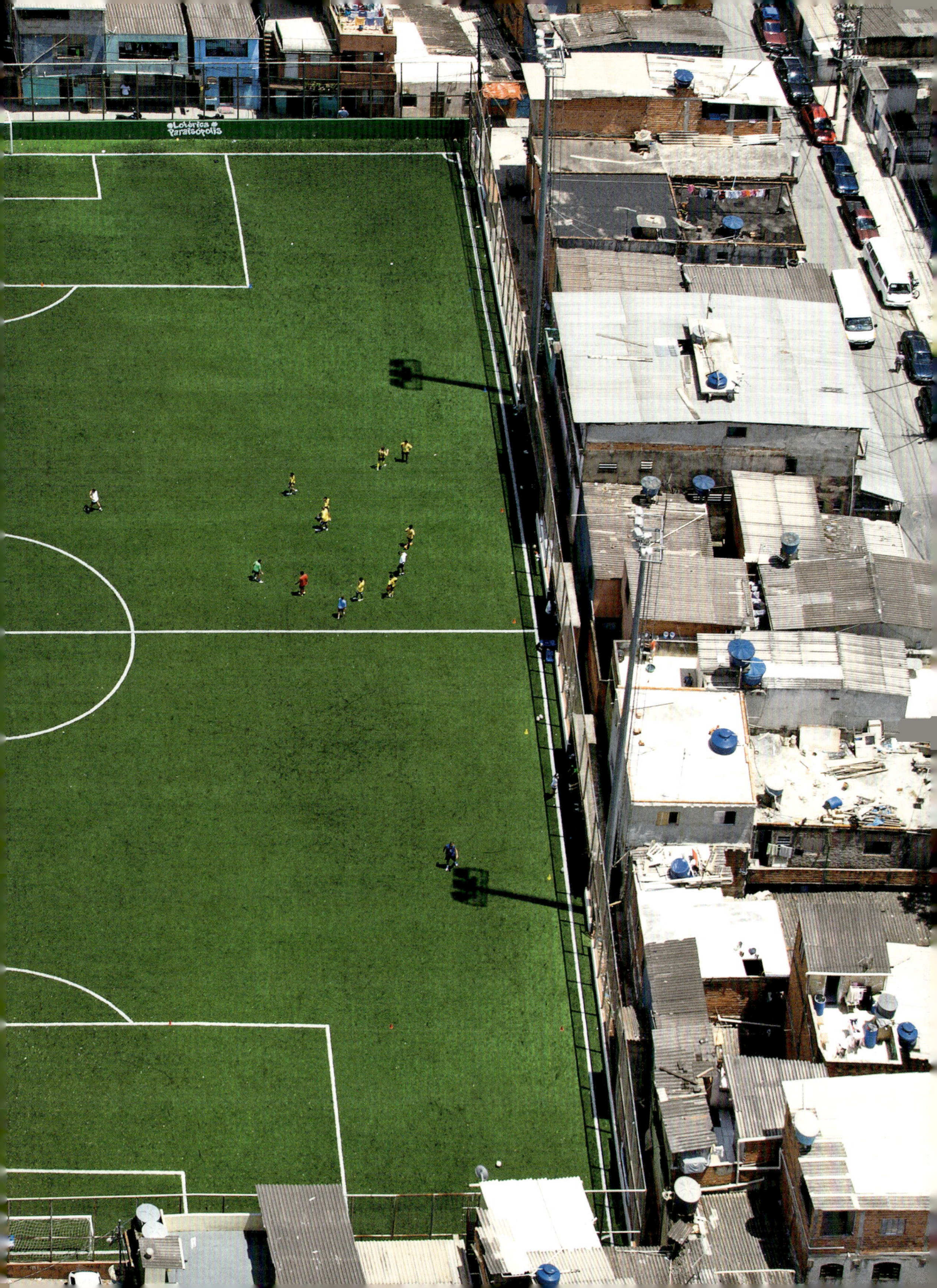
Lotérica
Paraisópolis

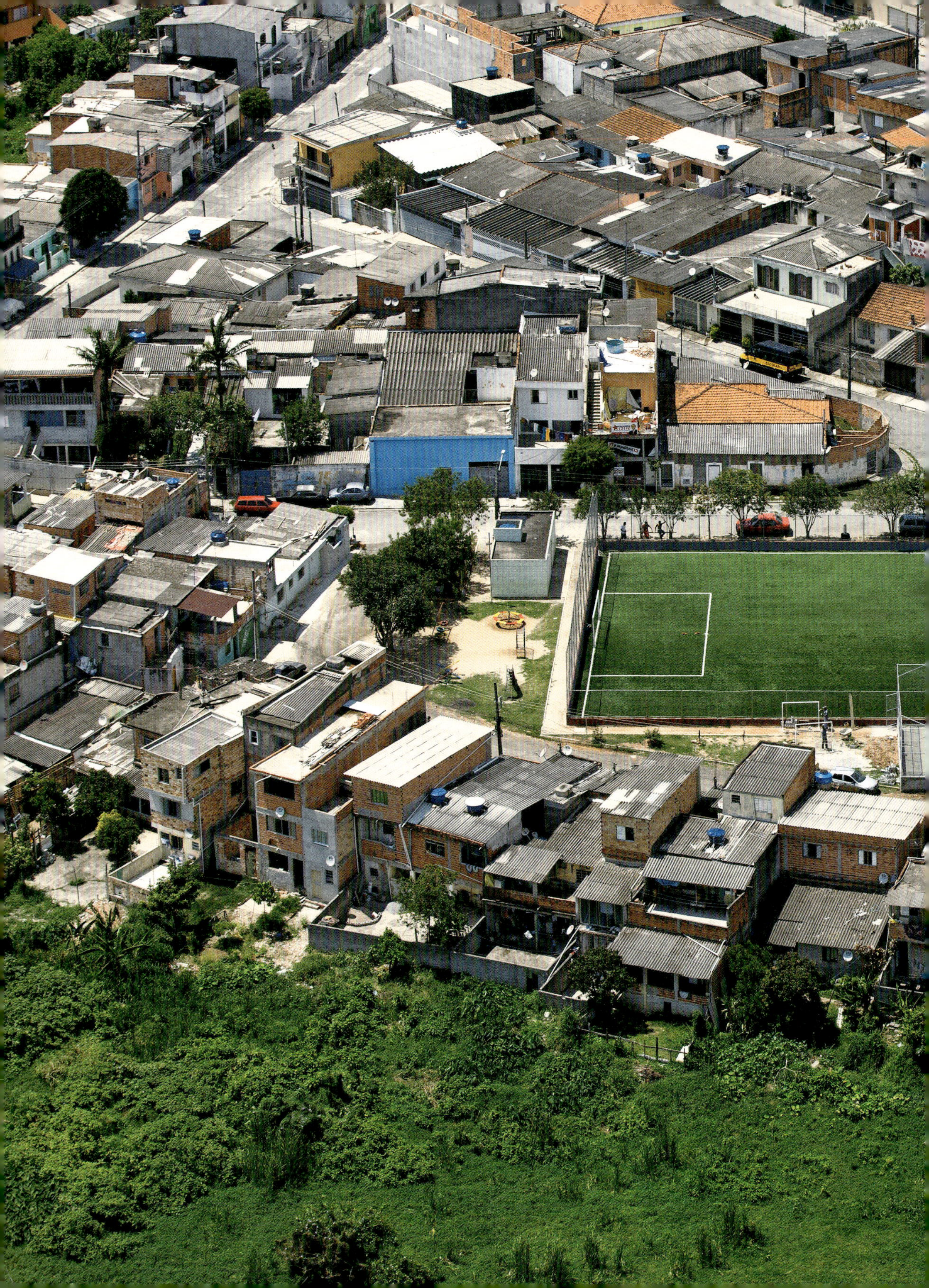

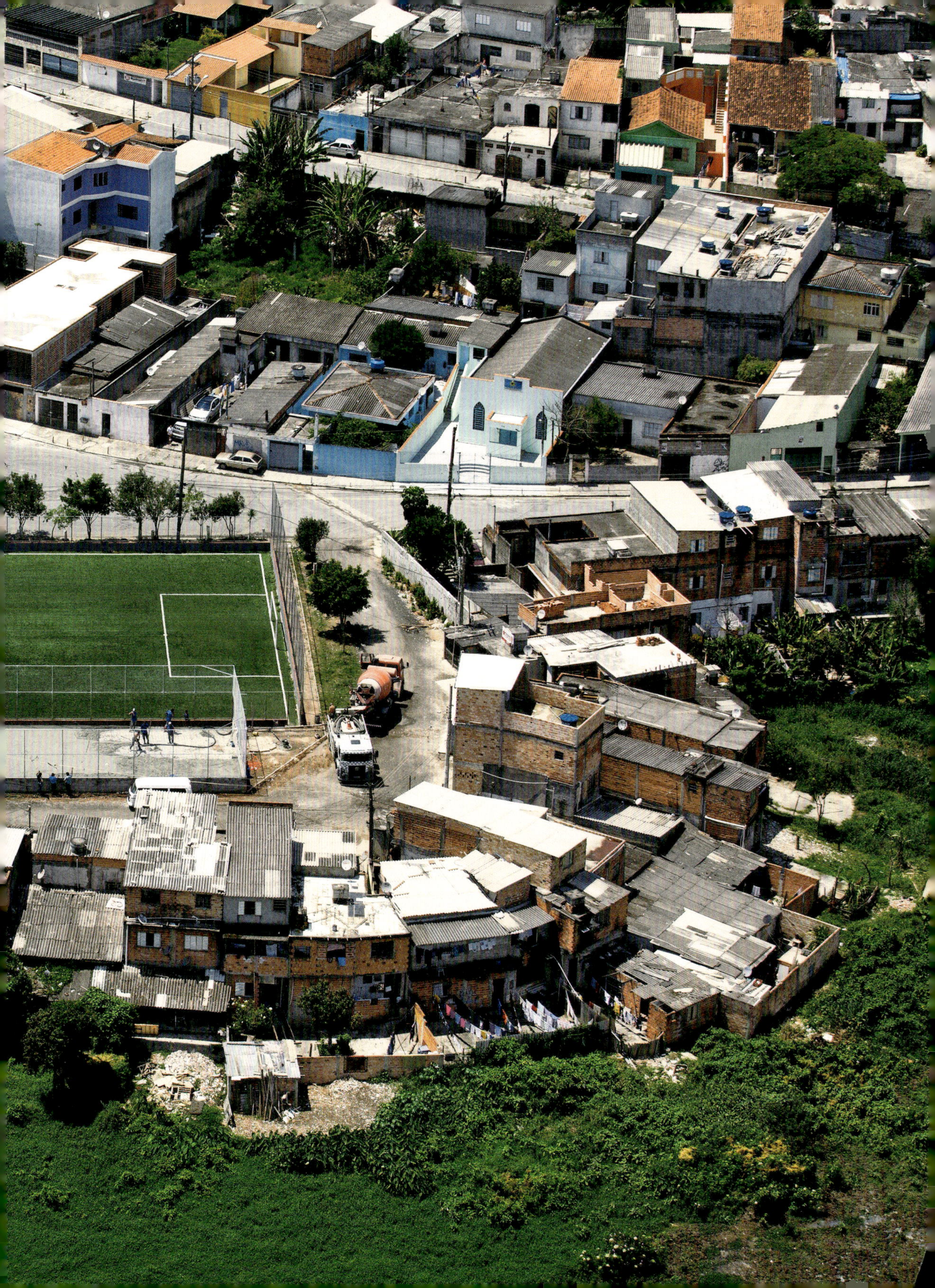

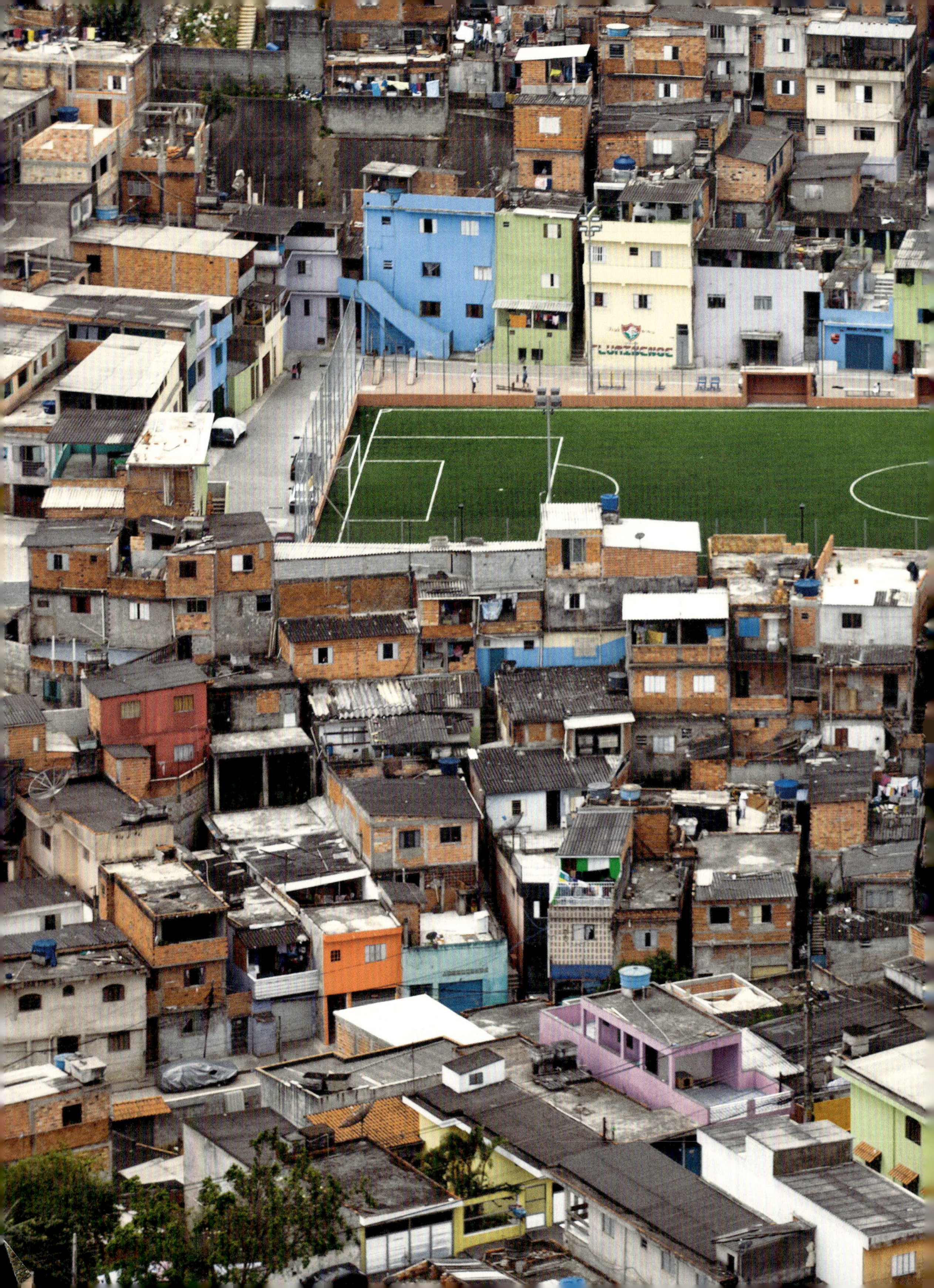

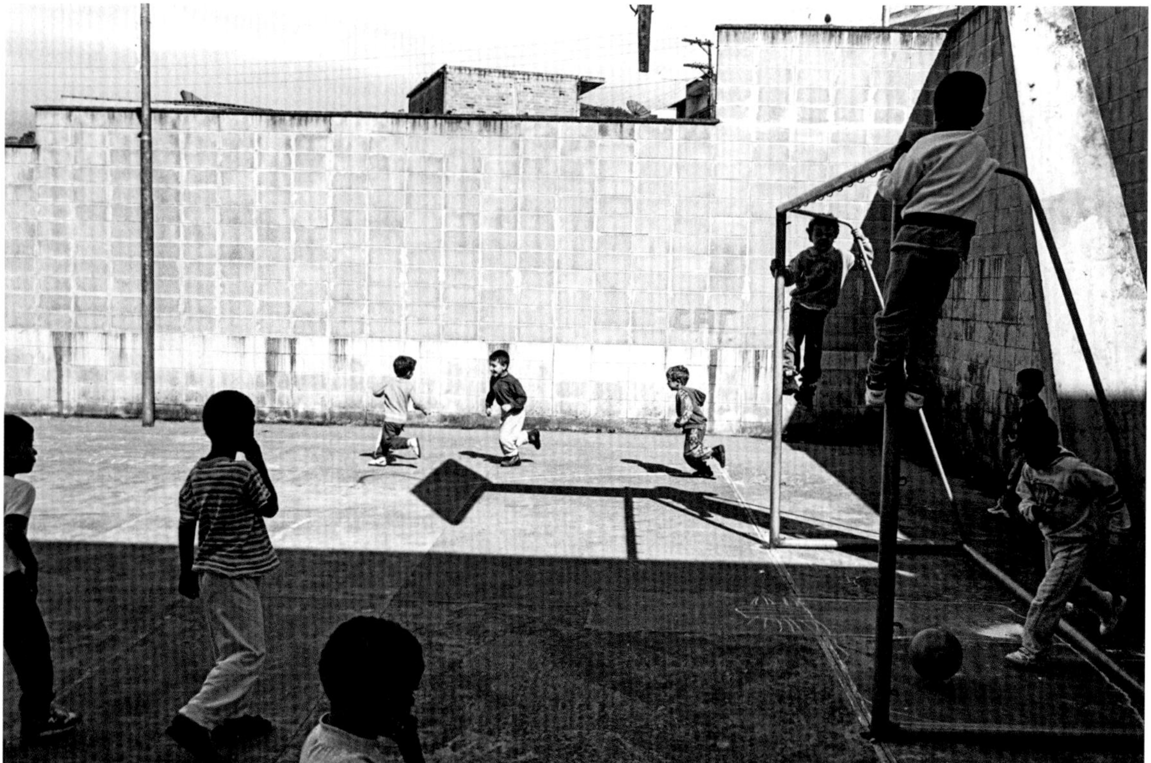

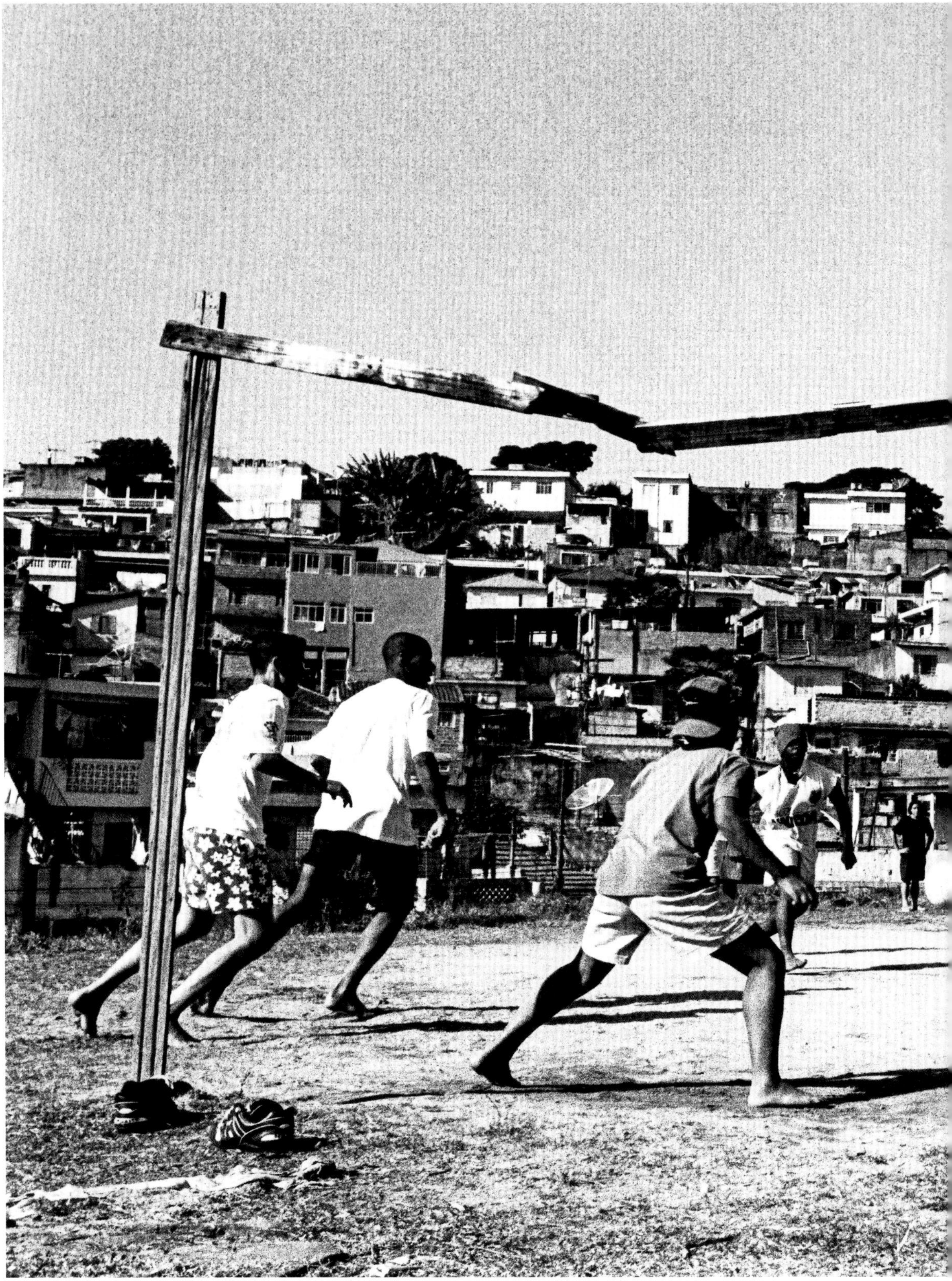

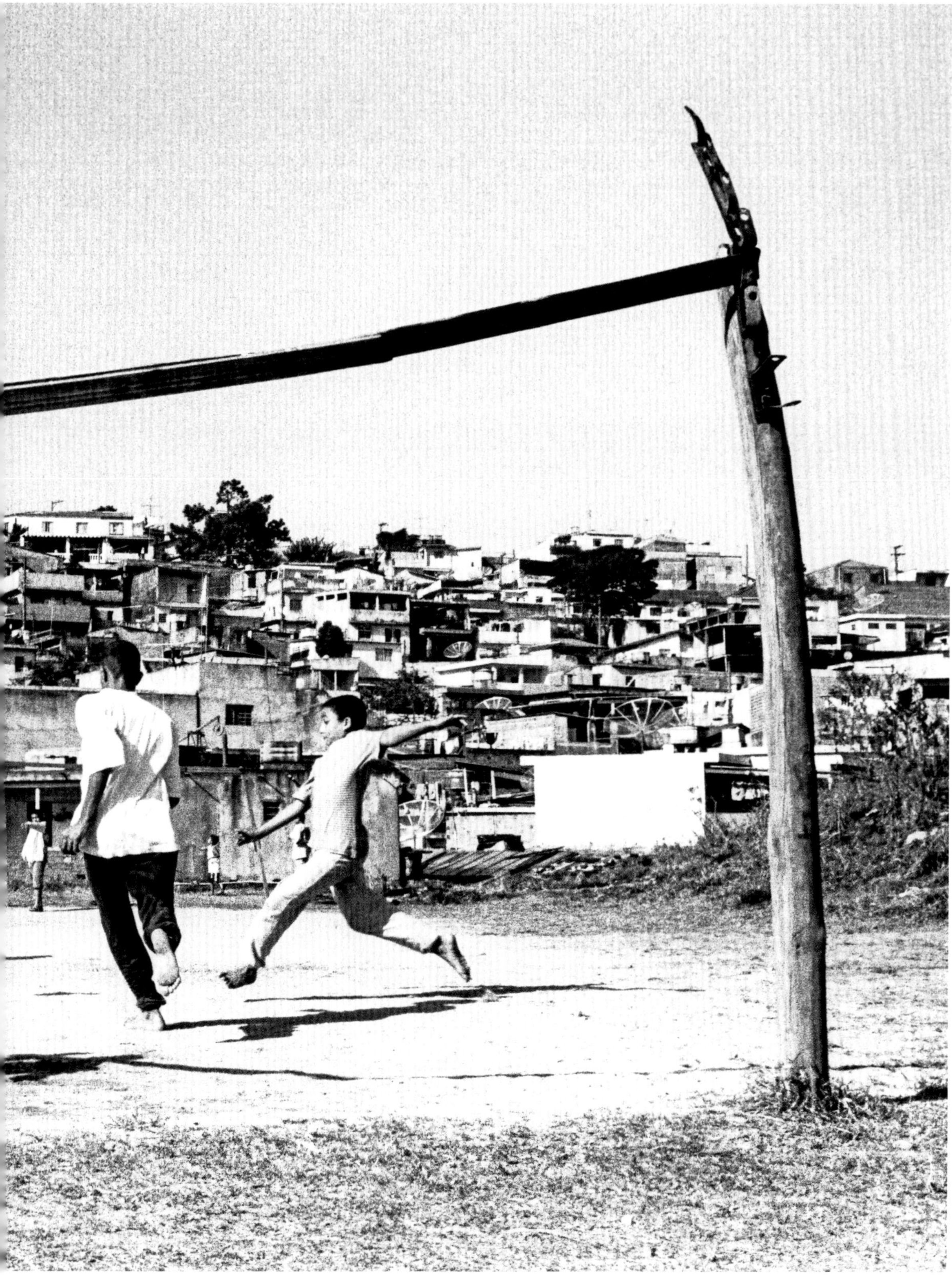

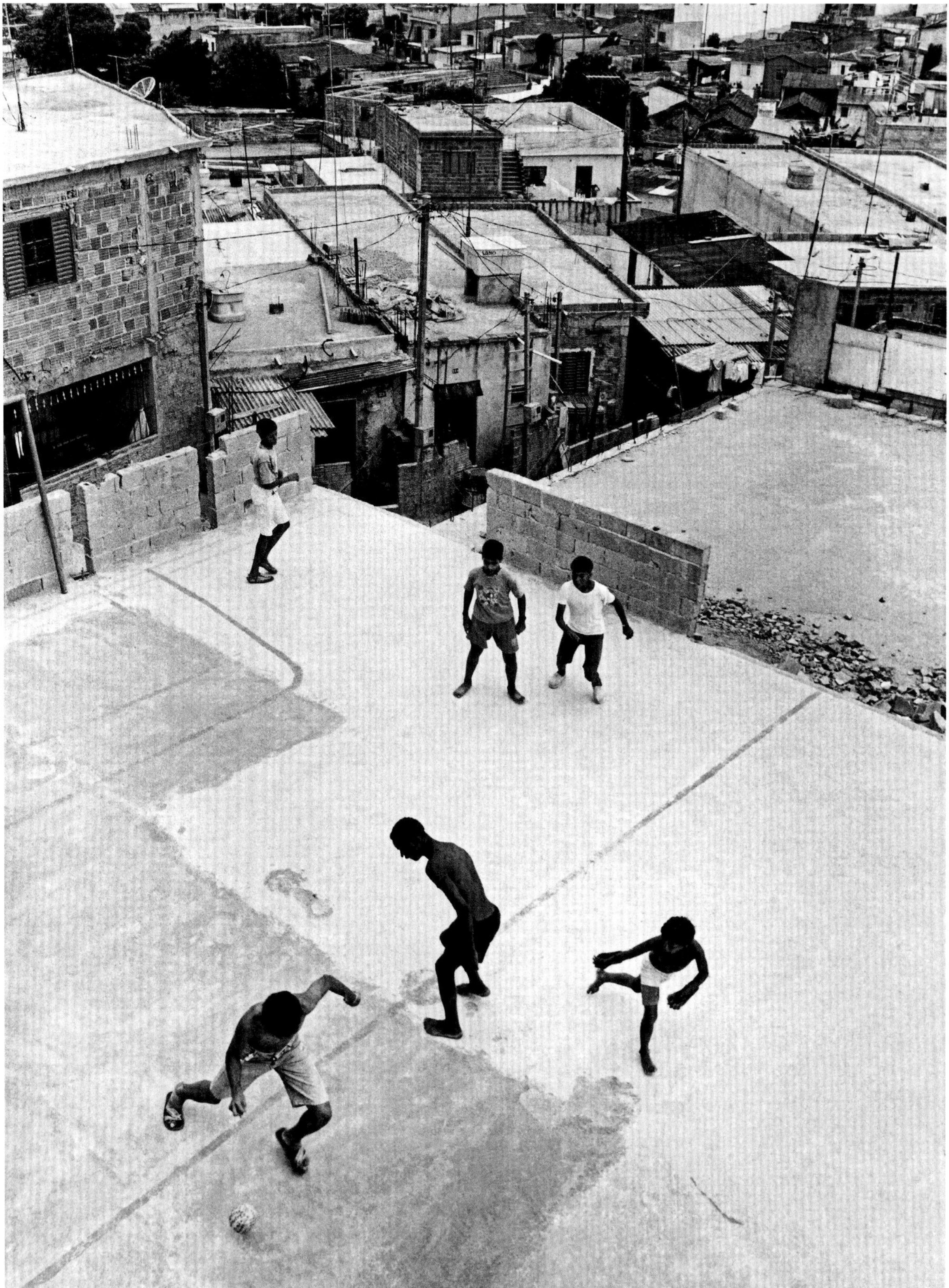

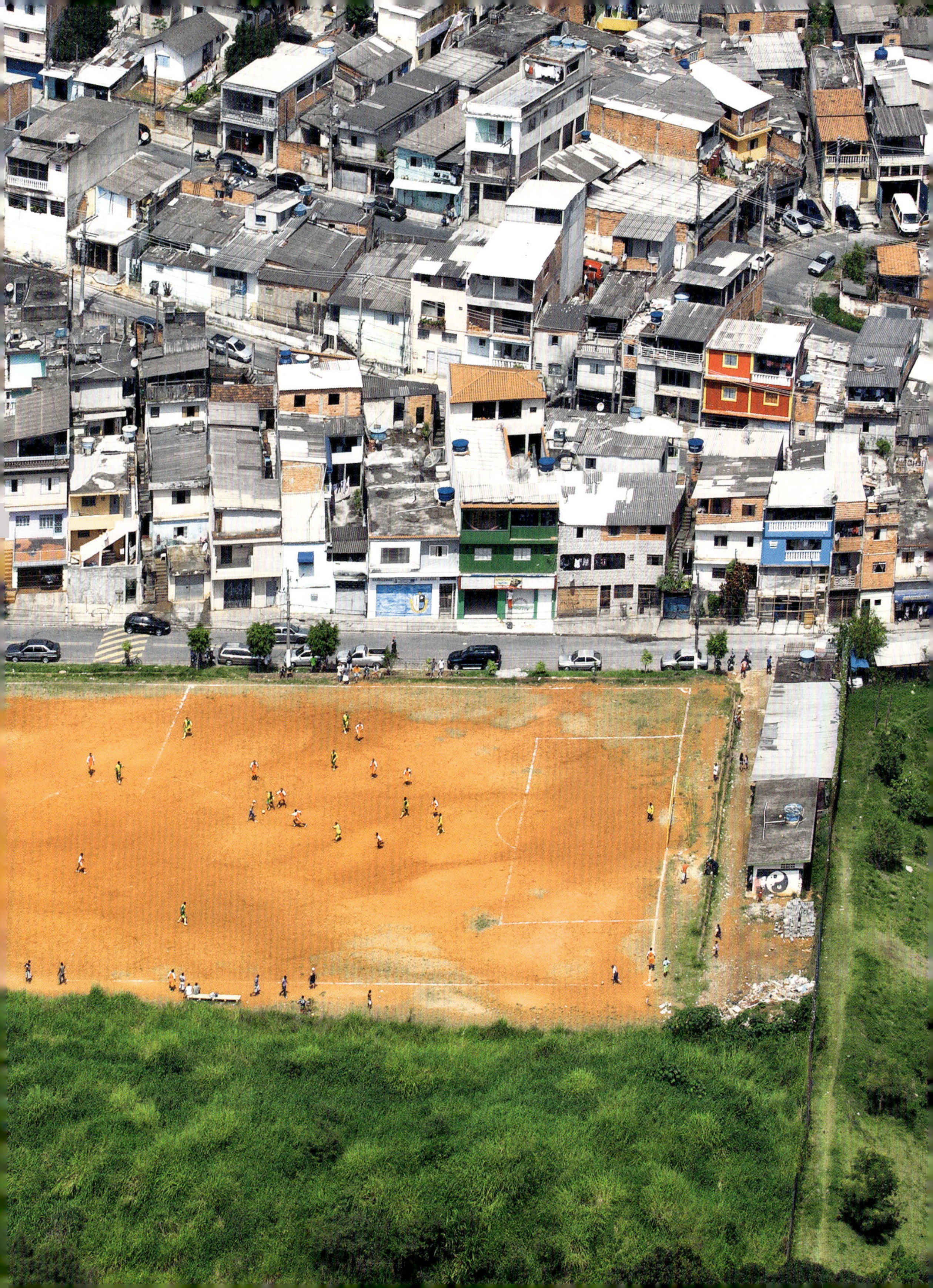

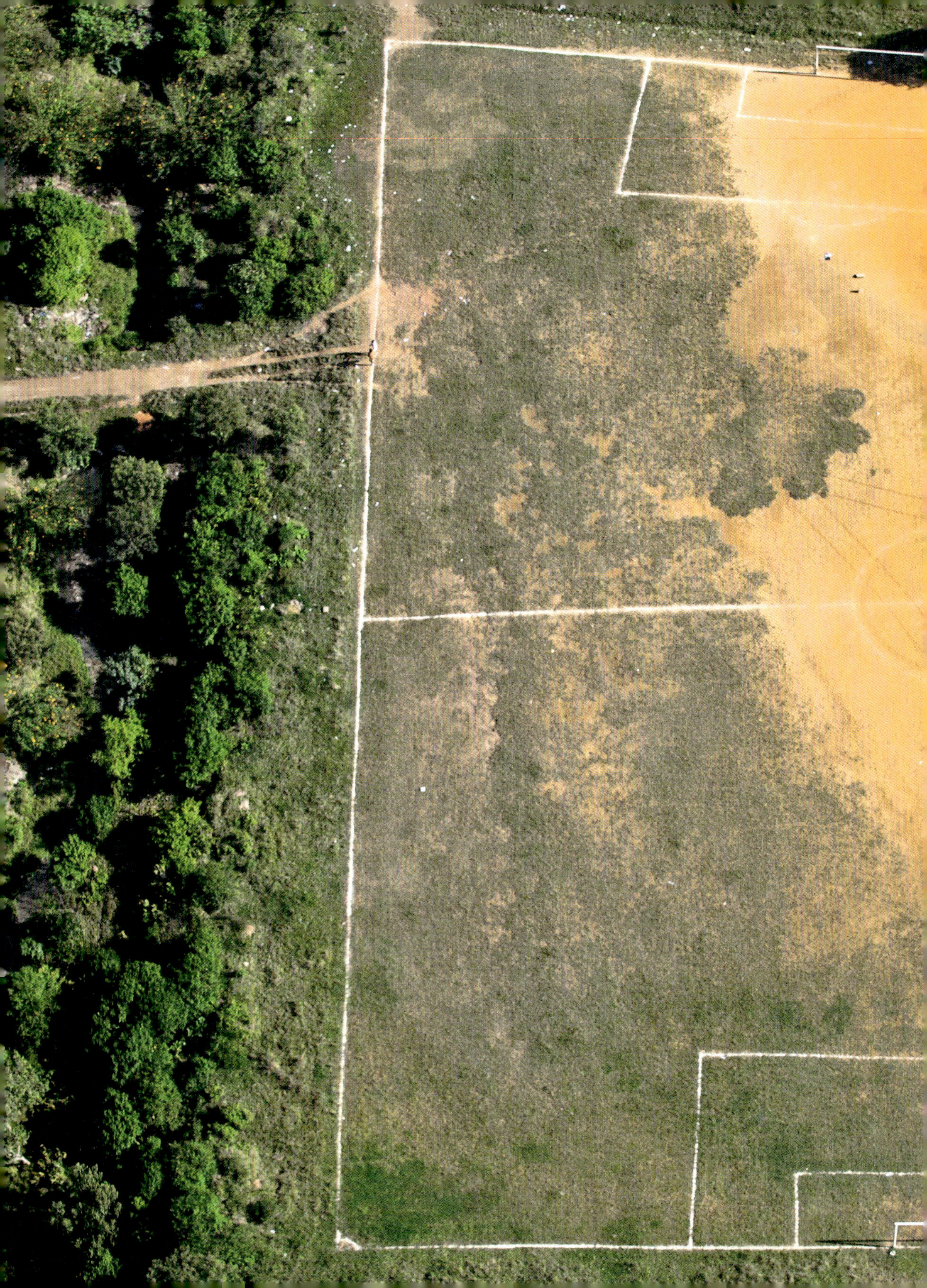

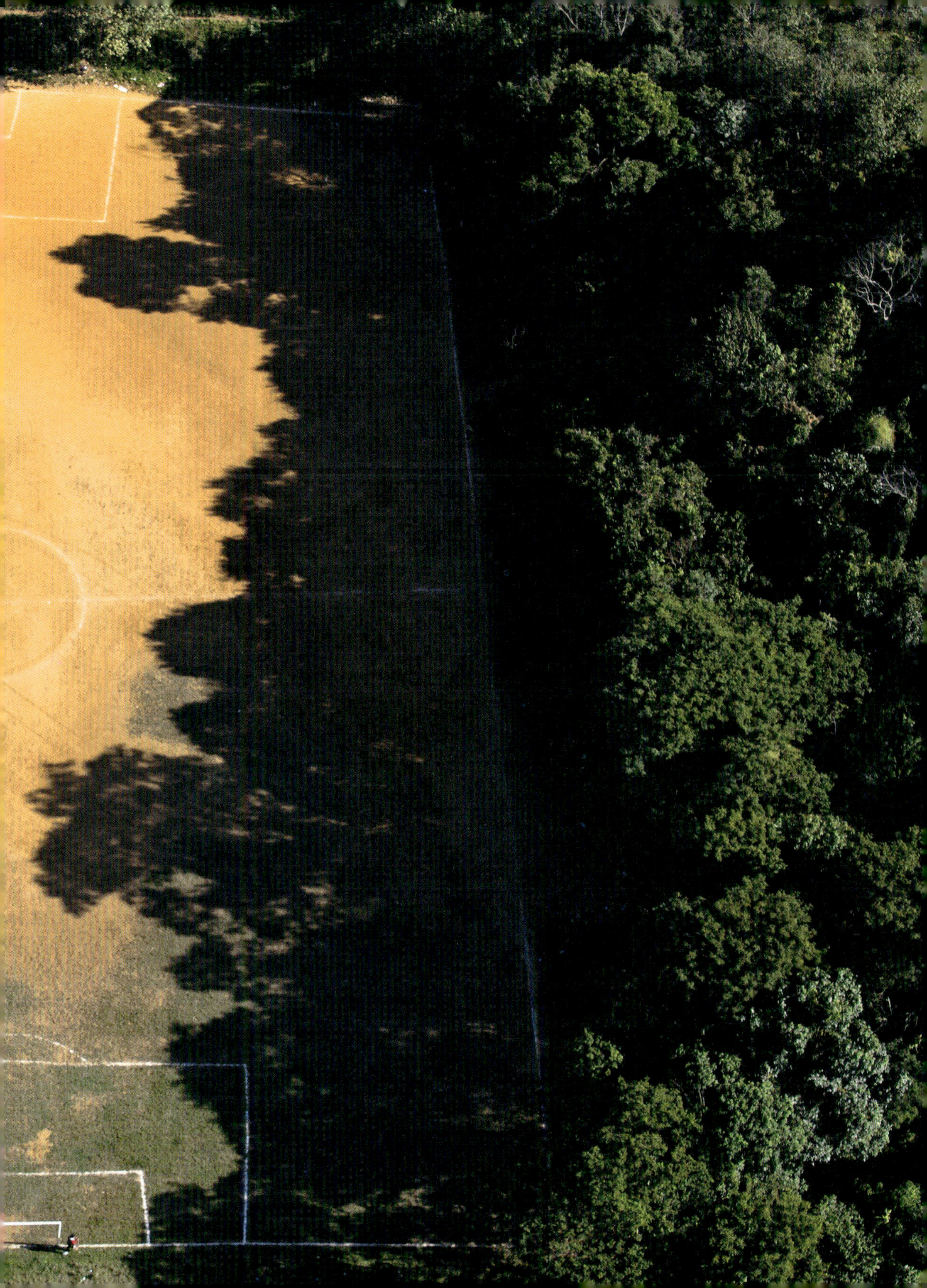

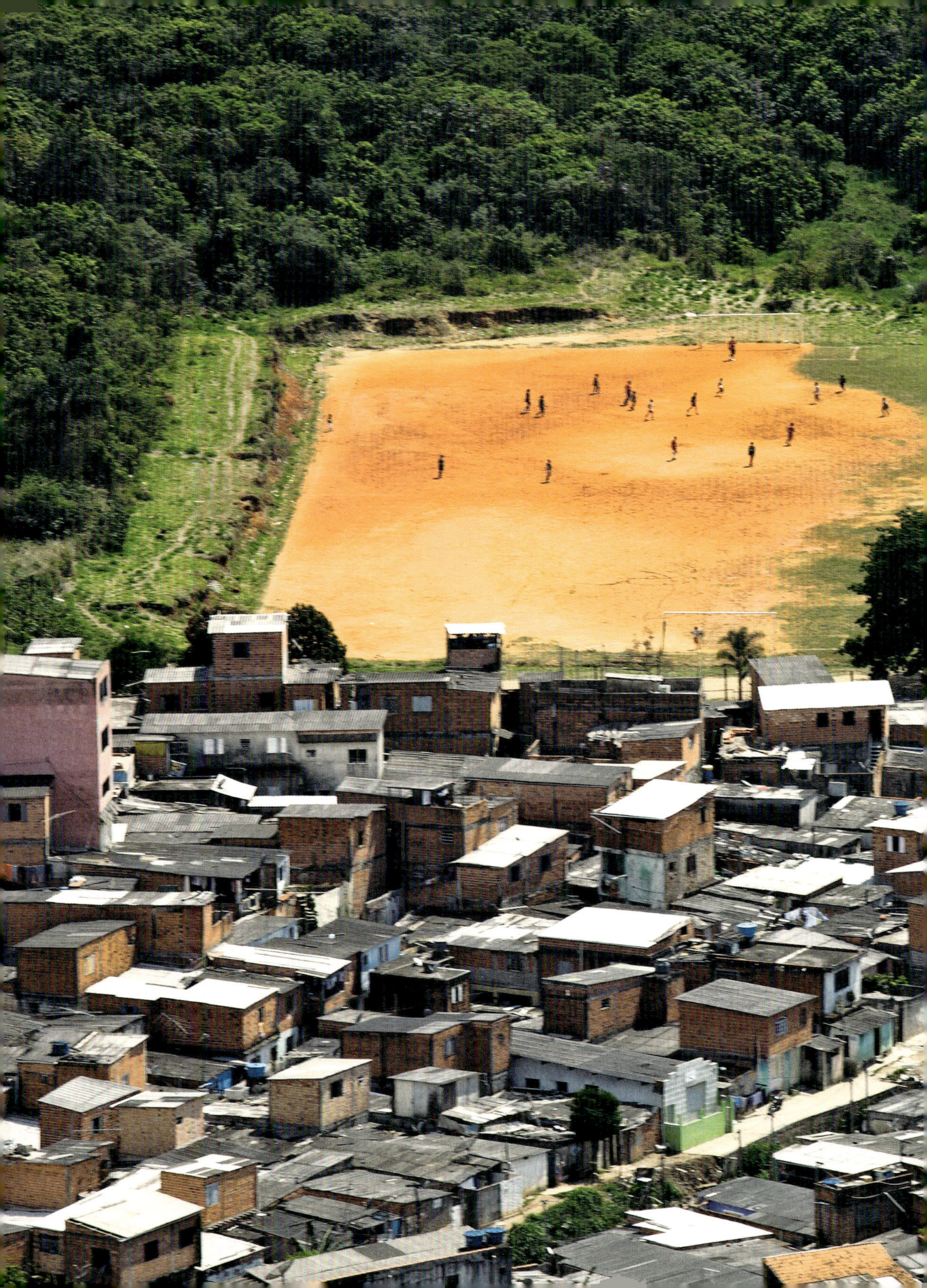

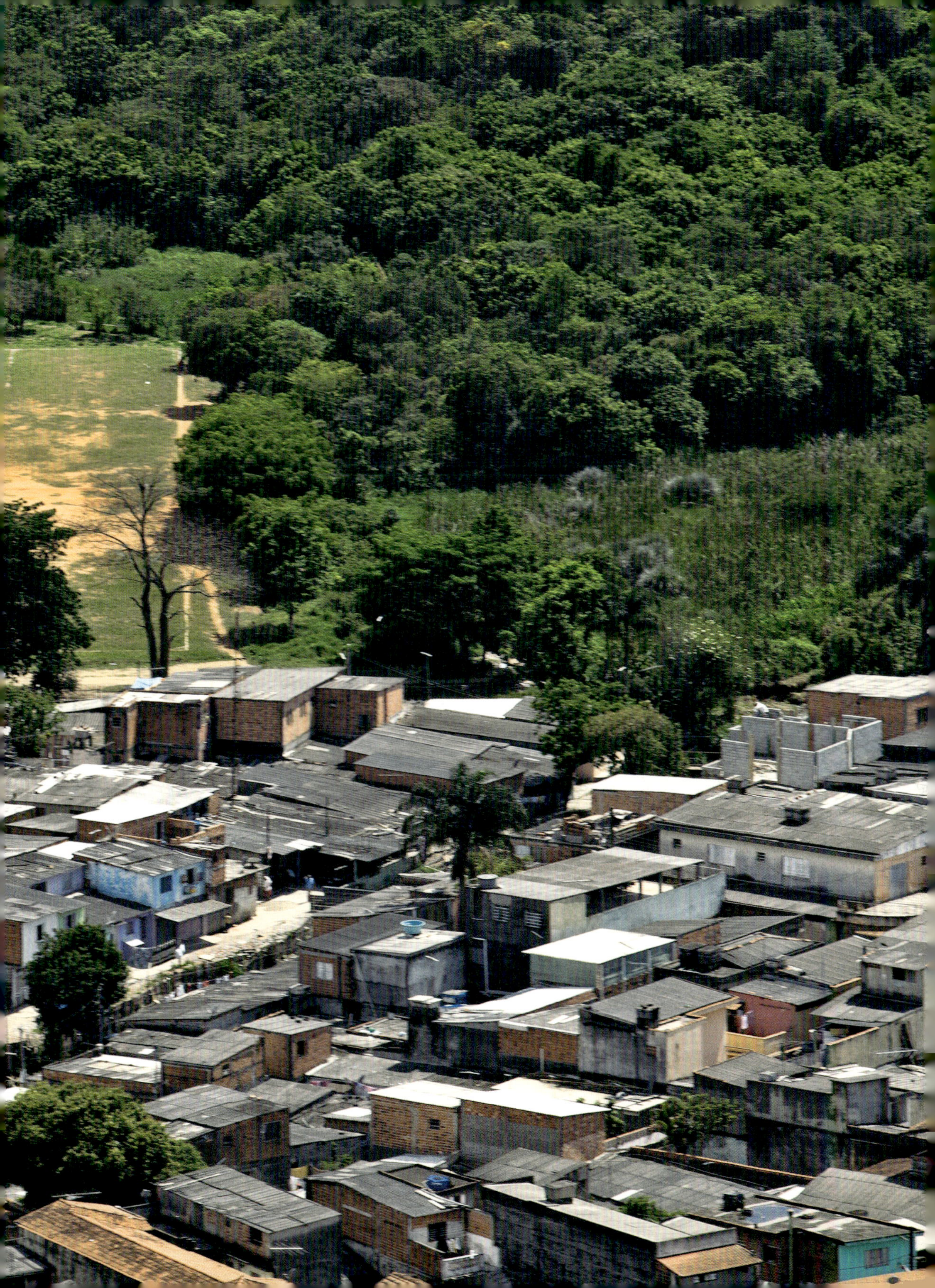

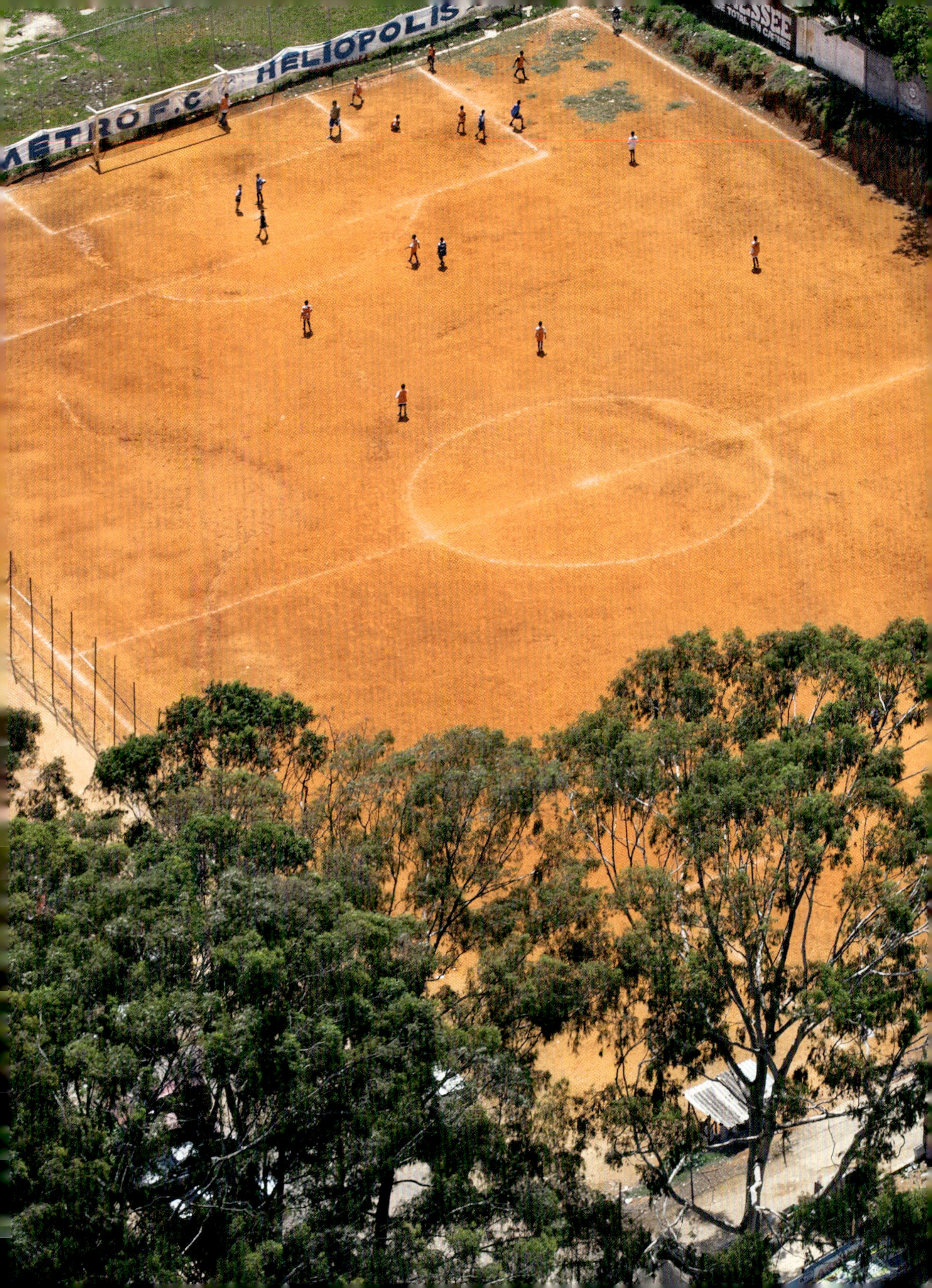
HELIOPOLIS

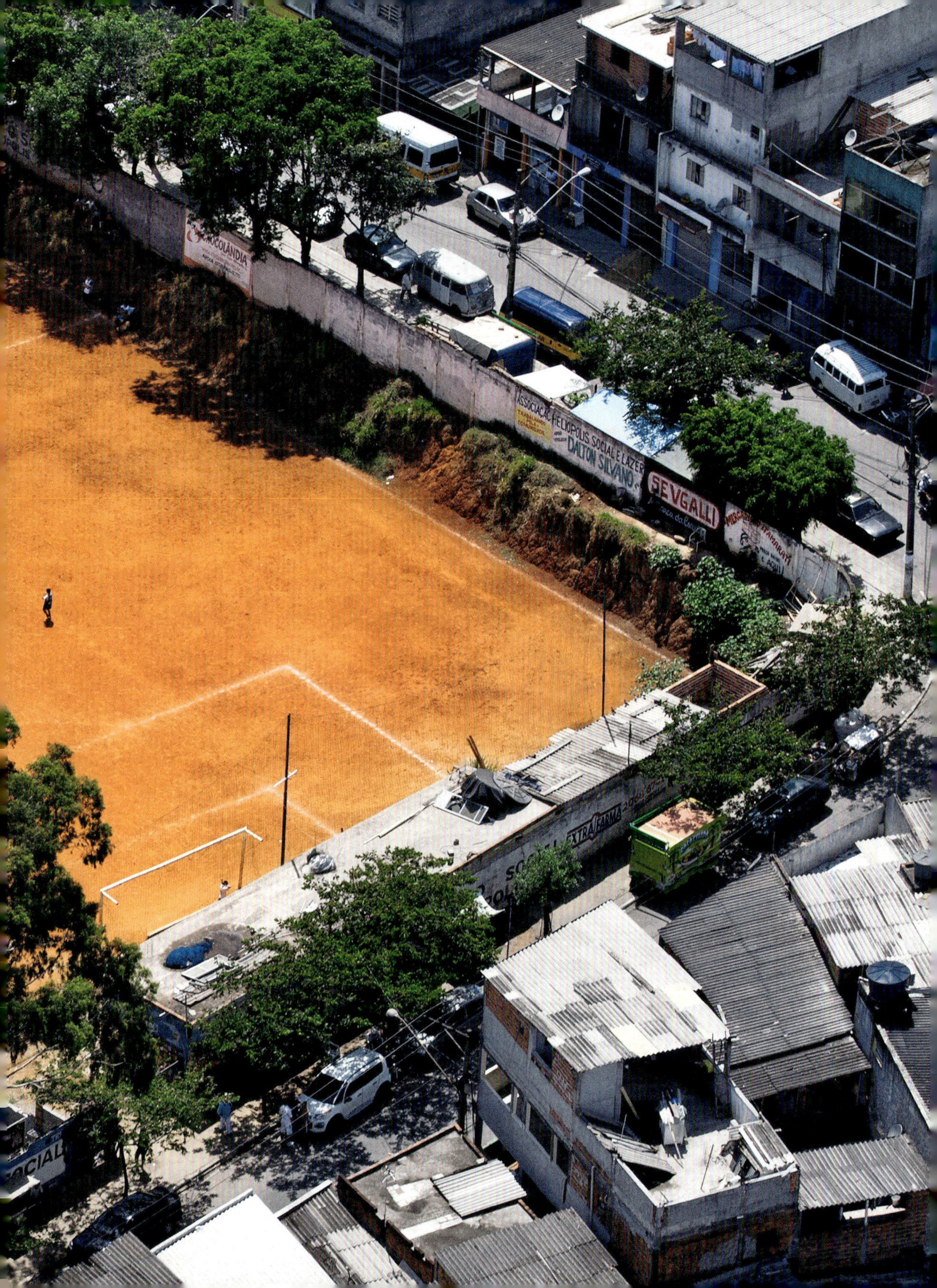
ASSOCIAÇÃ HELIÓPOLIS SOCIAL E LAZER
DALTON SILVANO
SEVGALLI
EXTRAFARMA

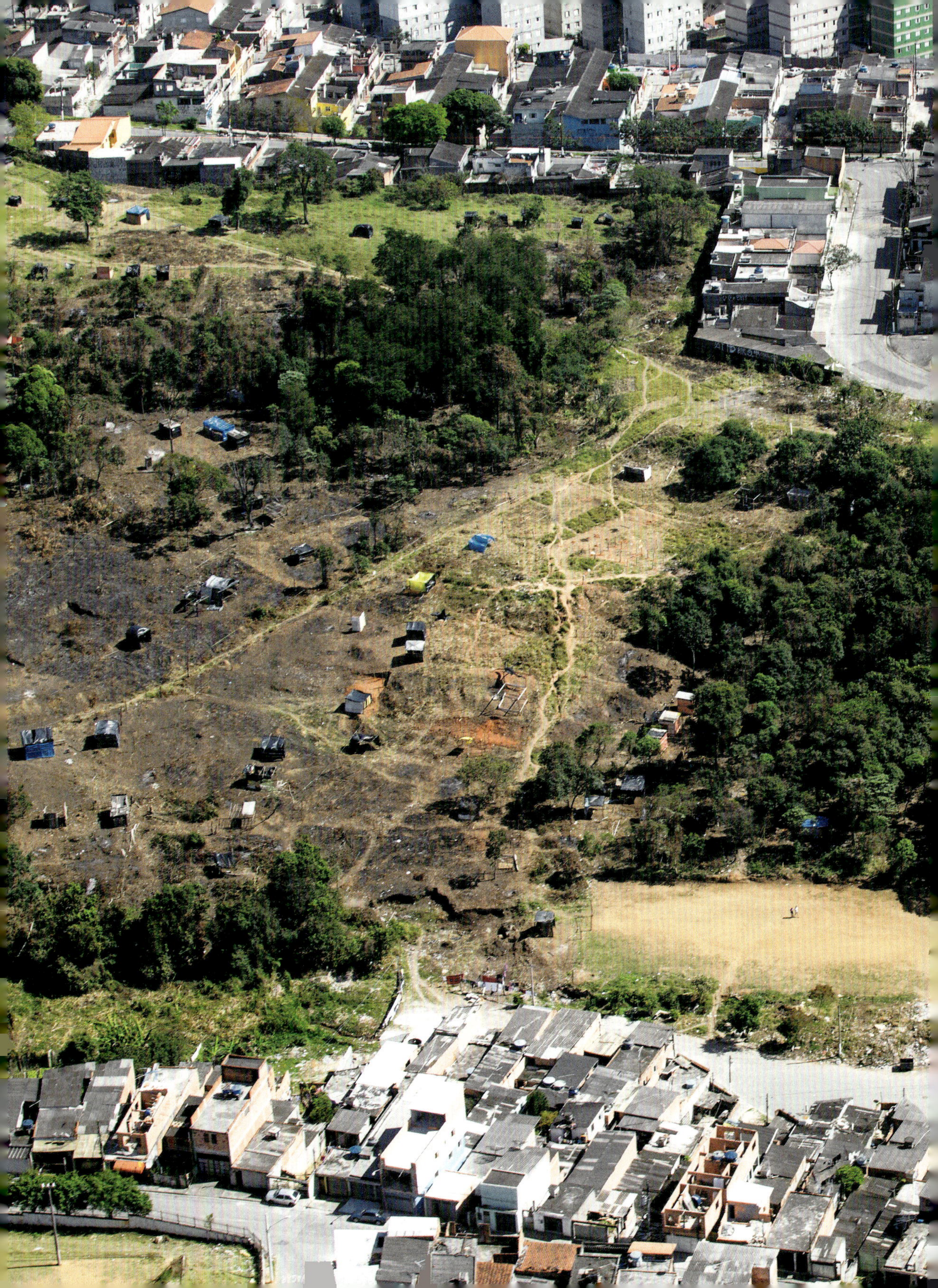

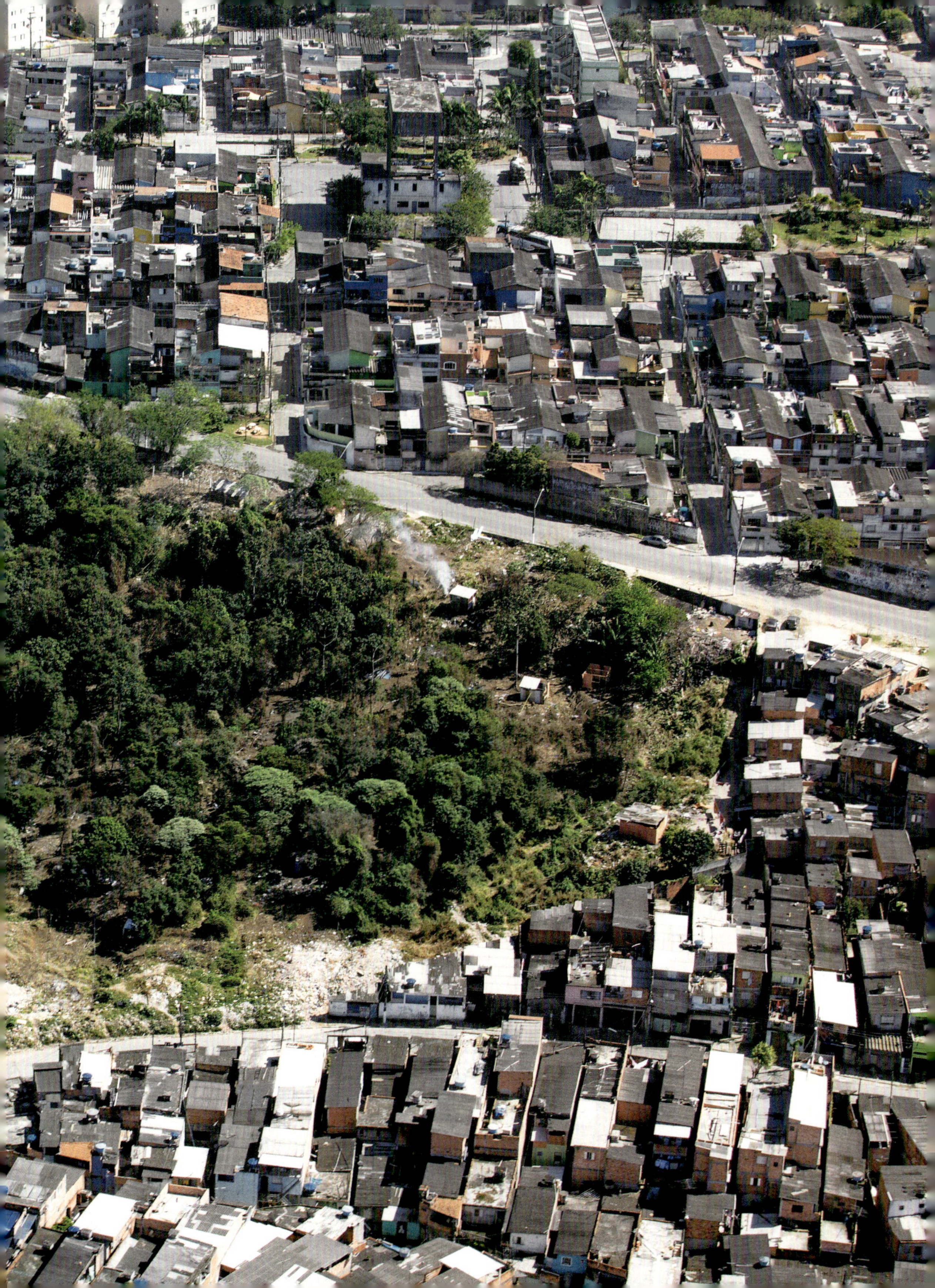

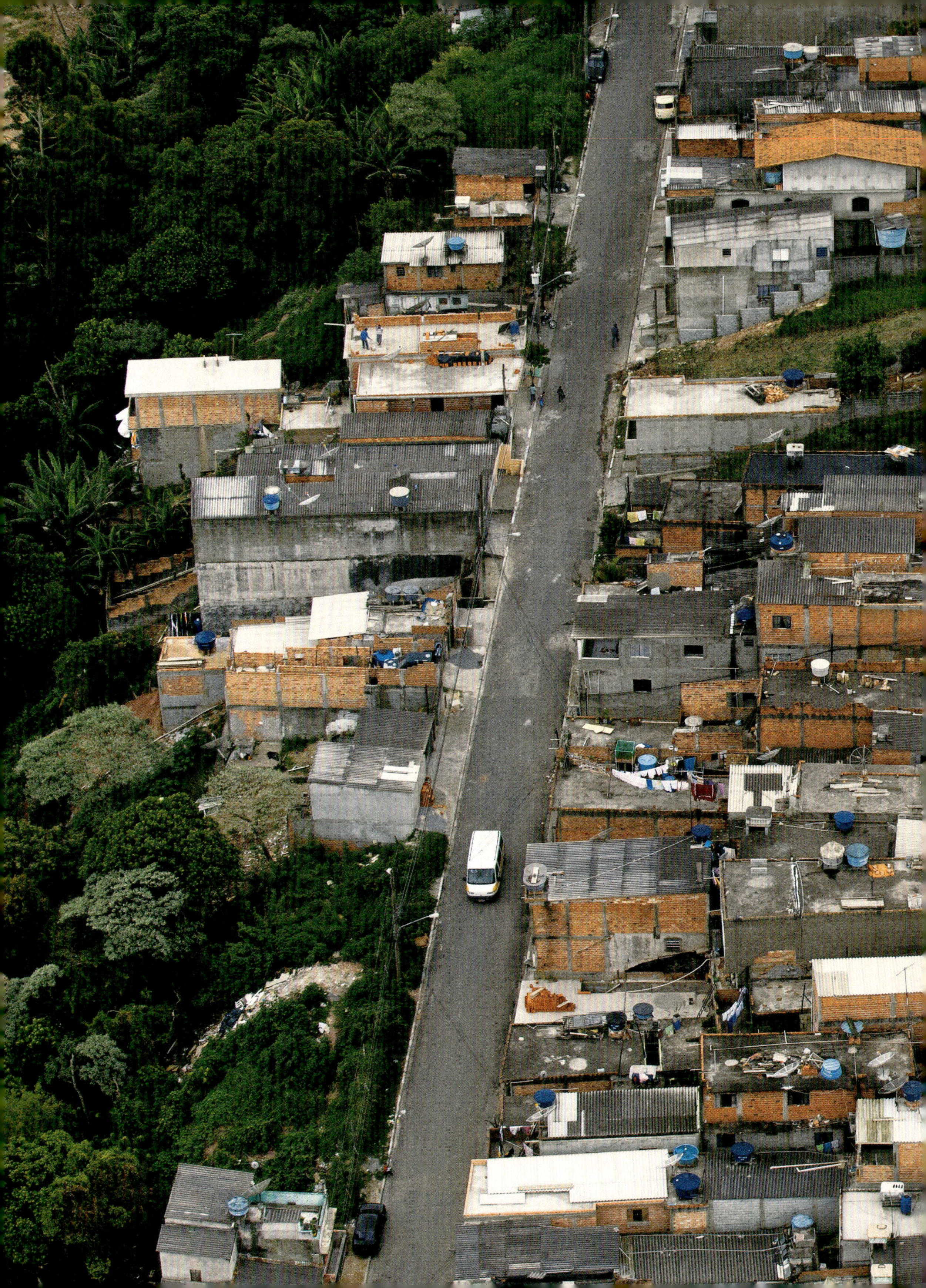

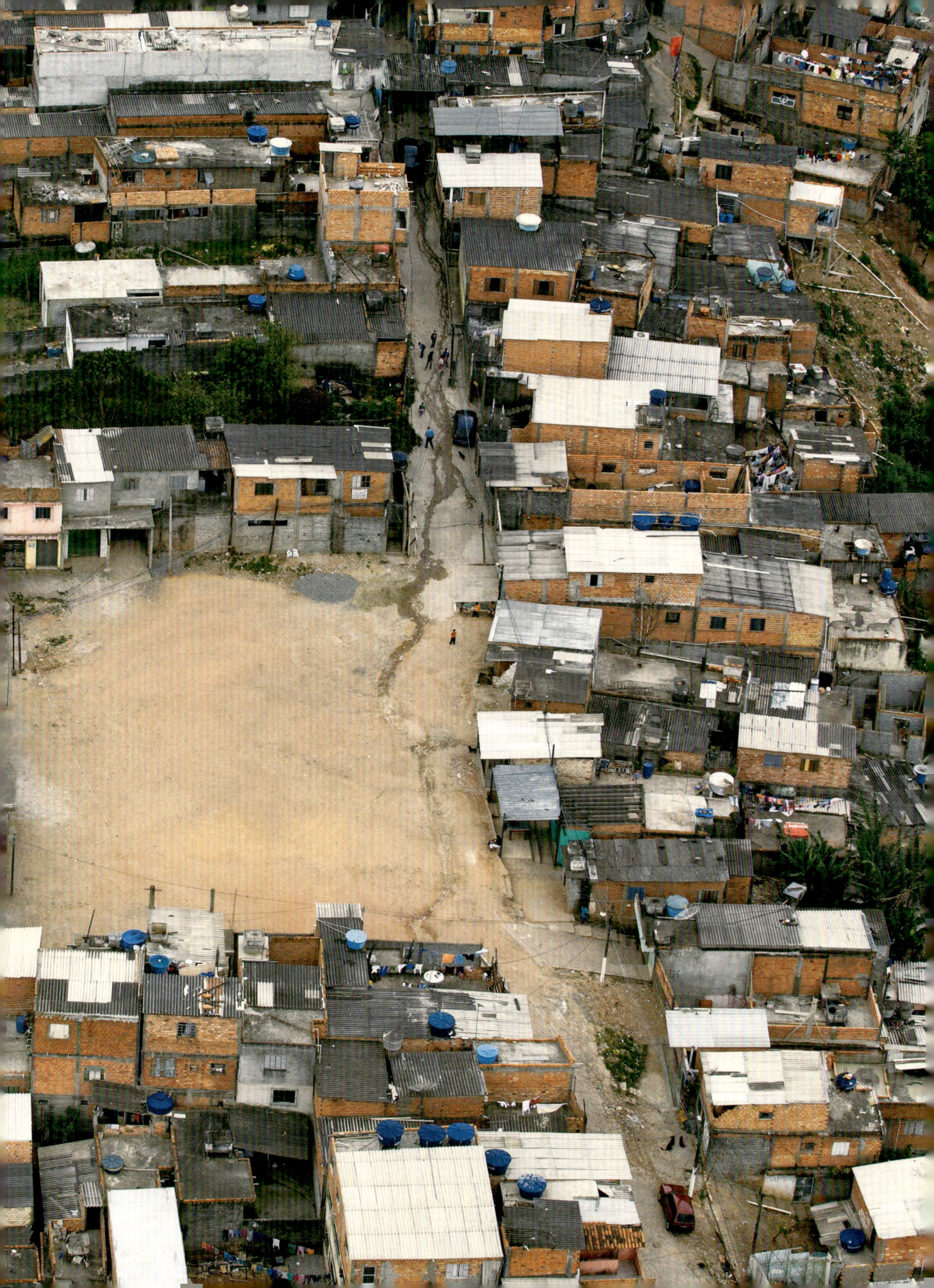

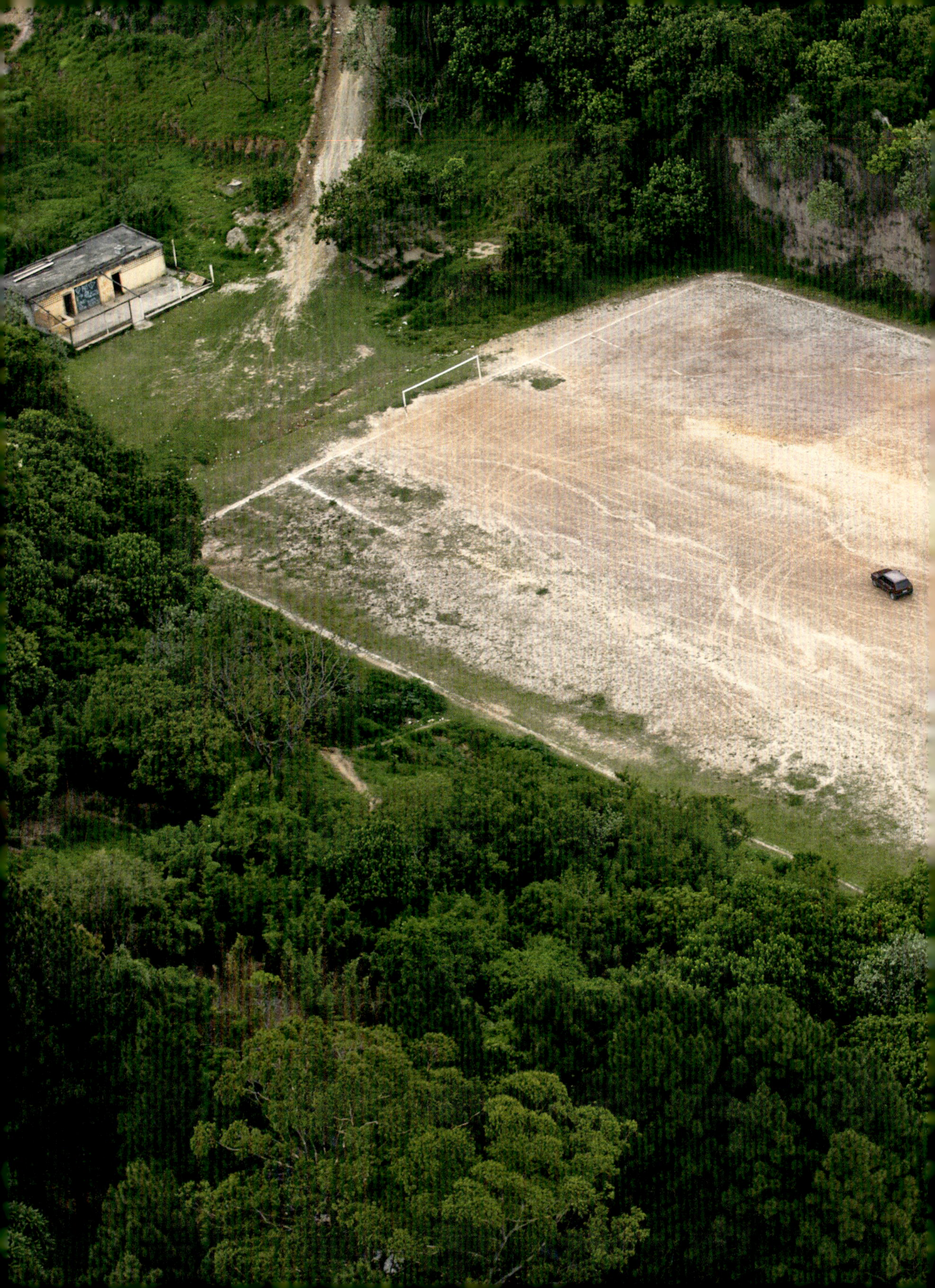

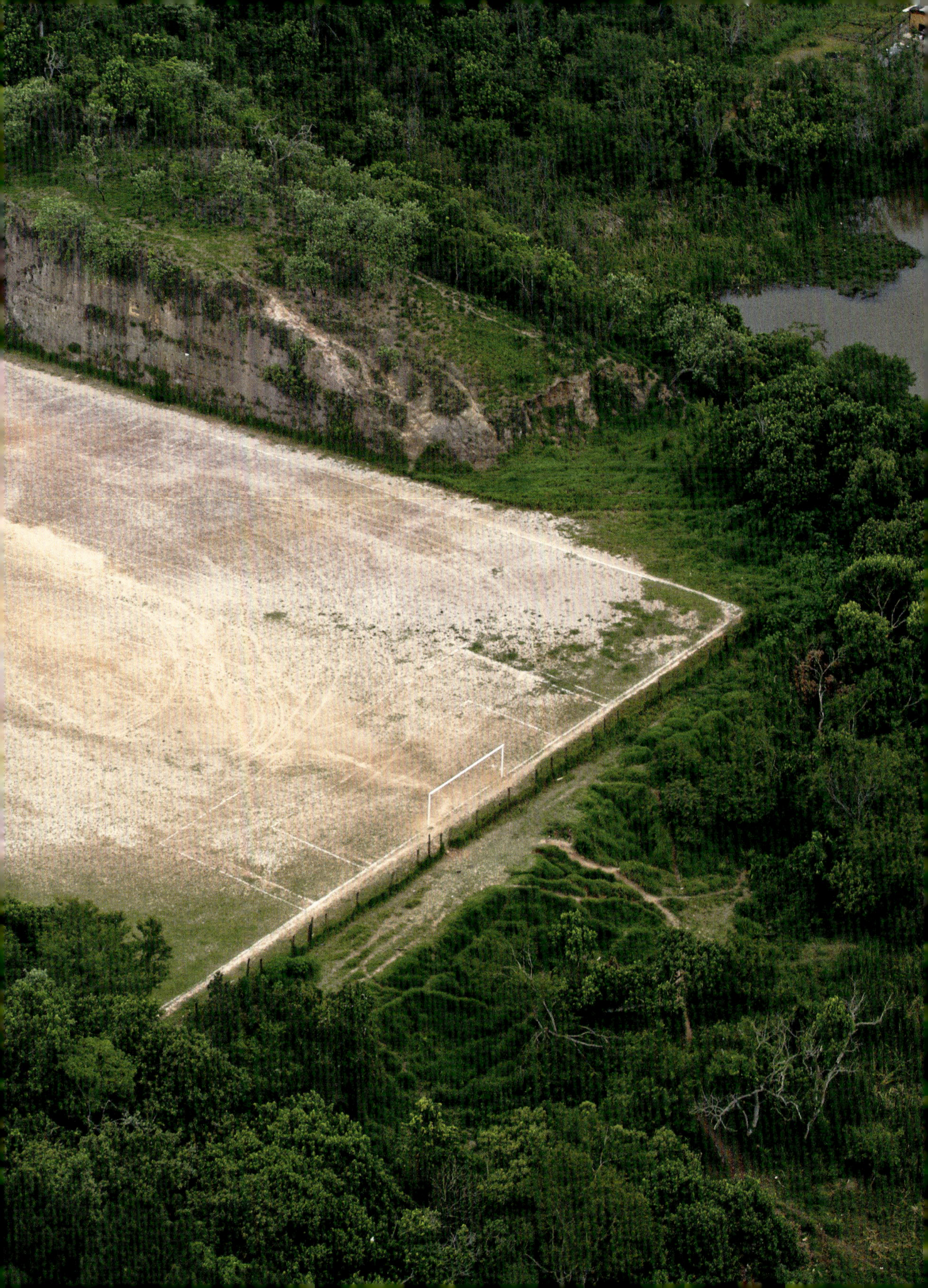

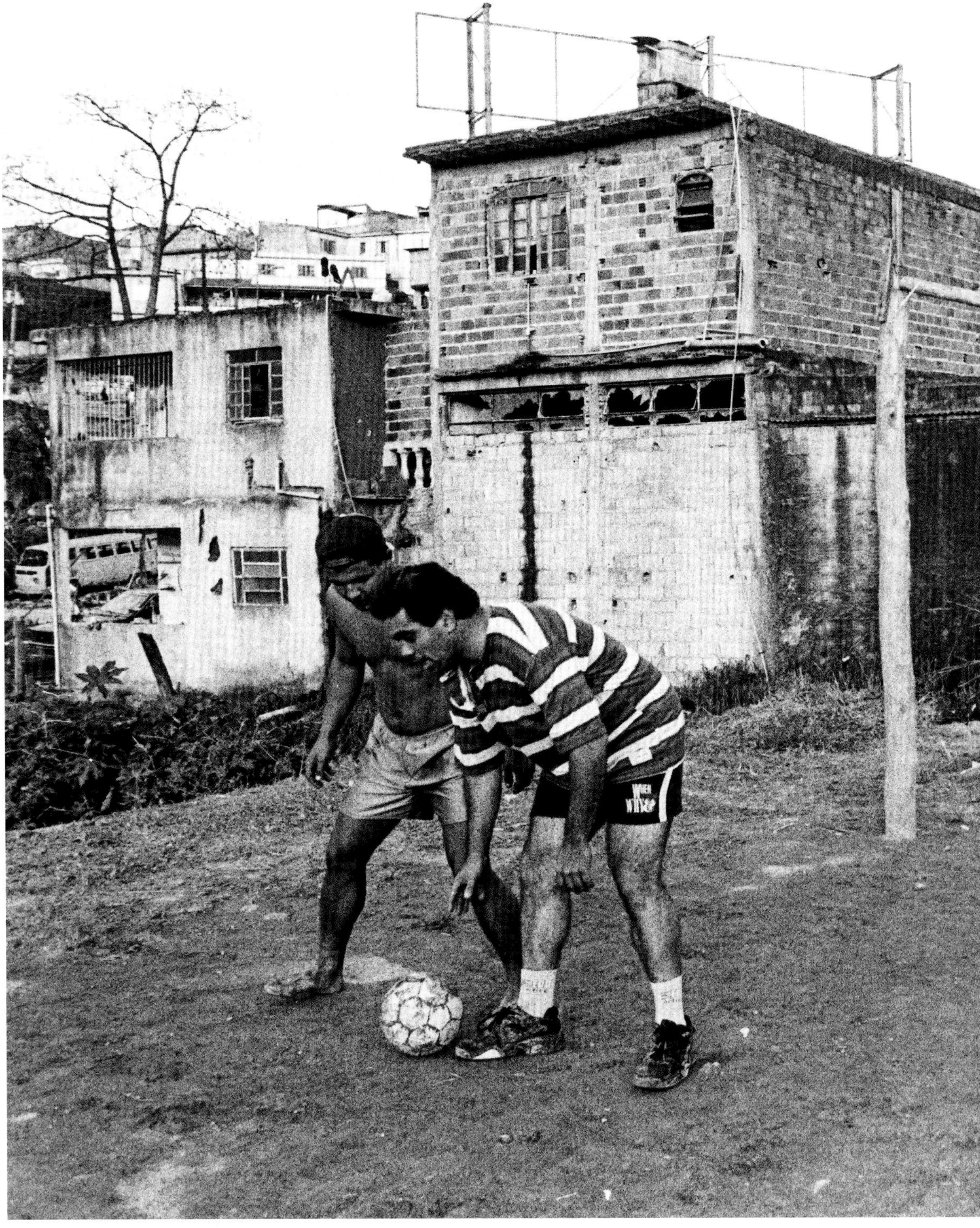

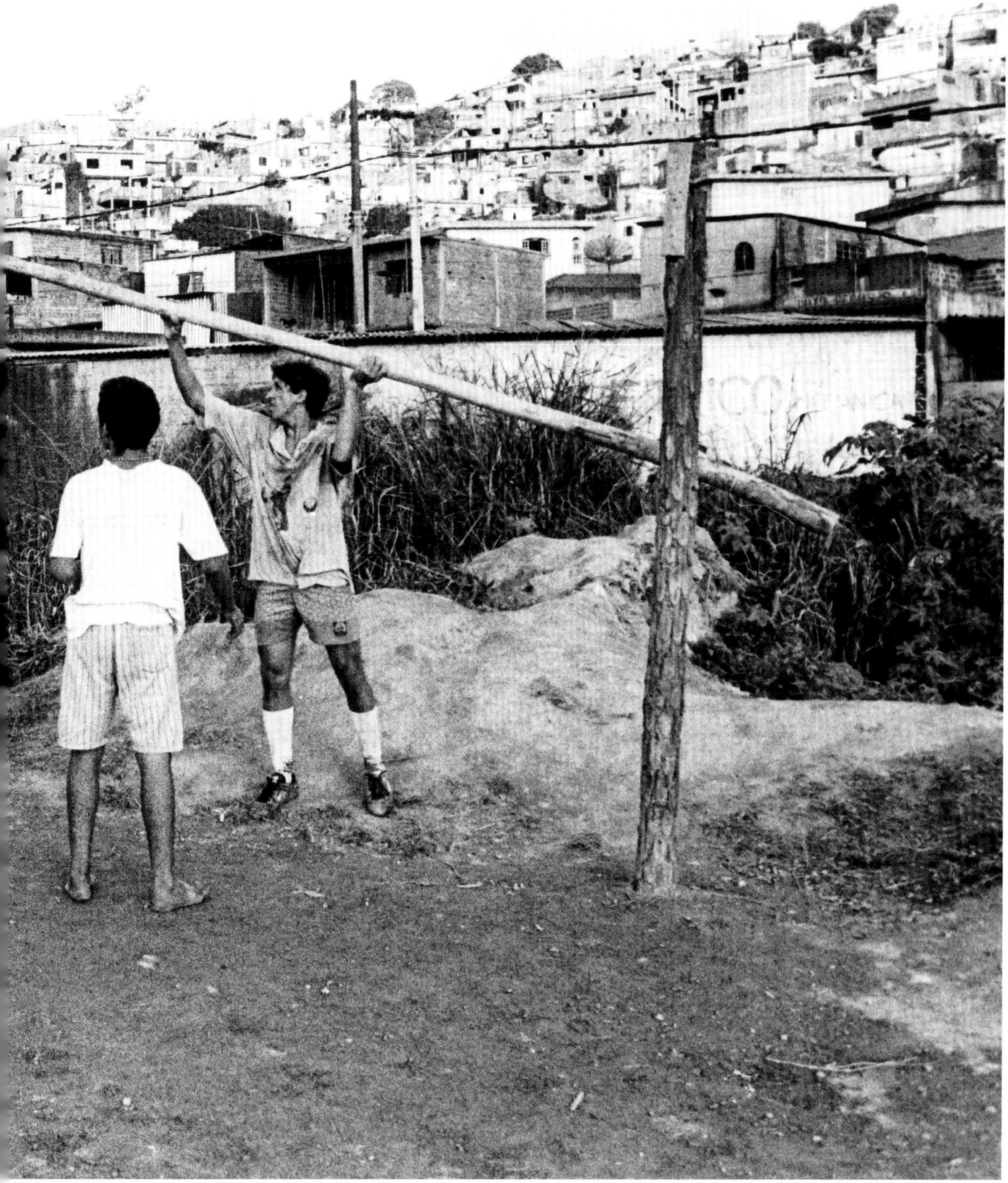

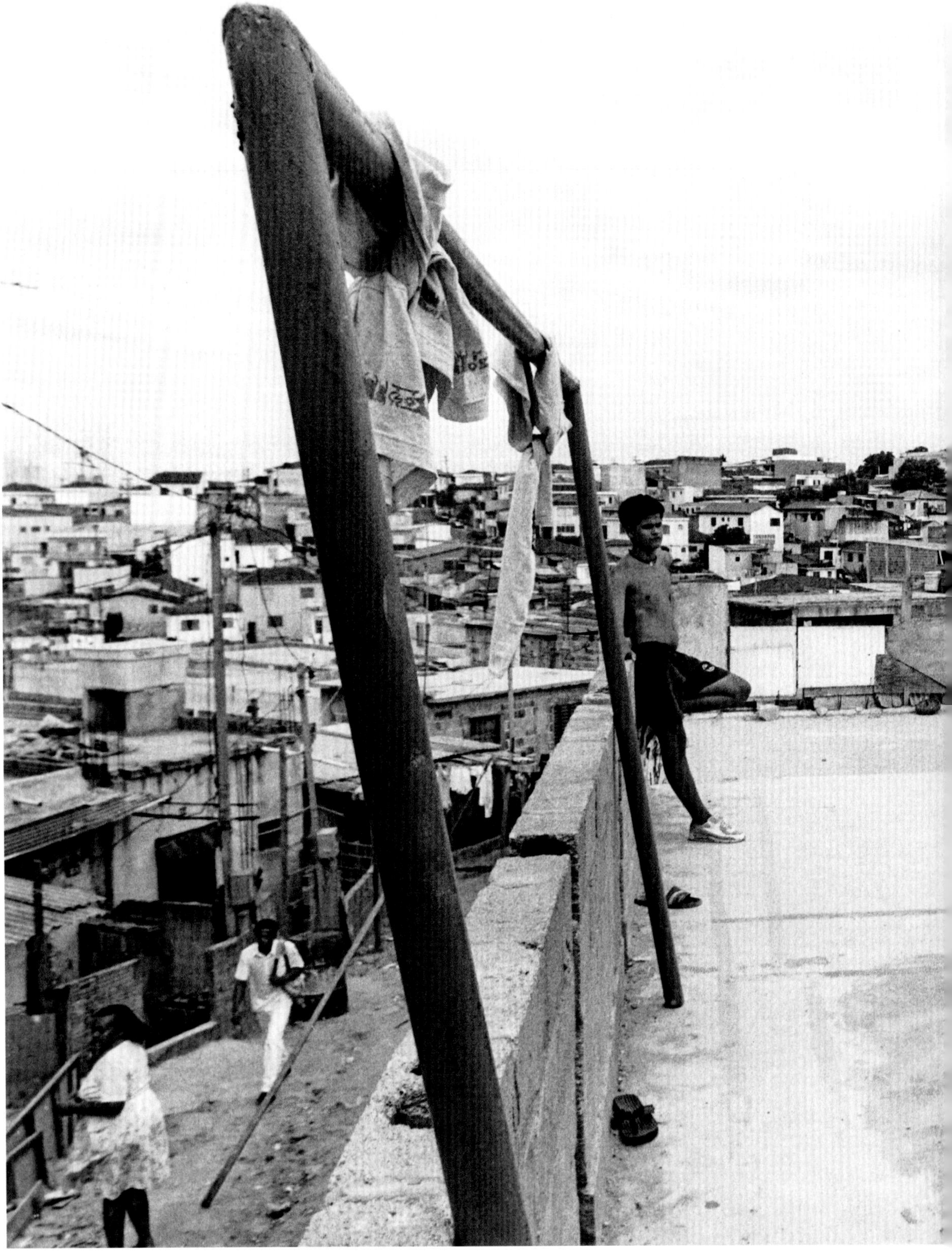

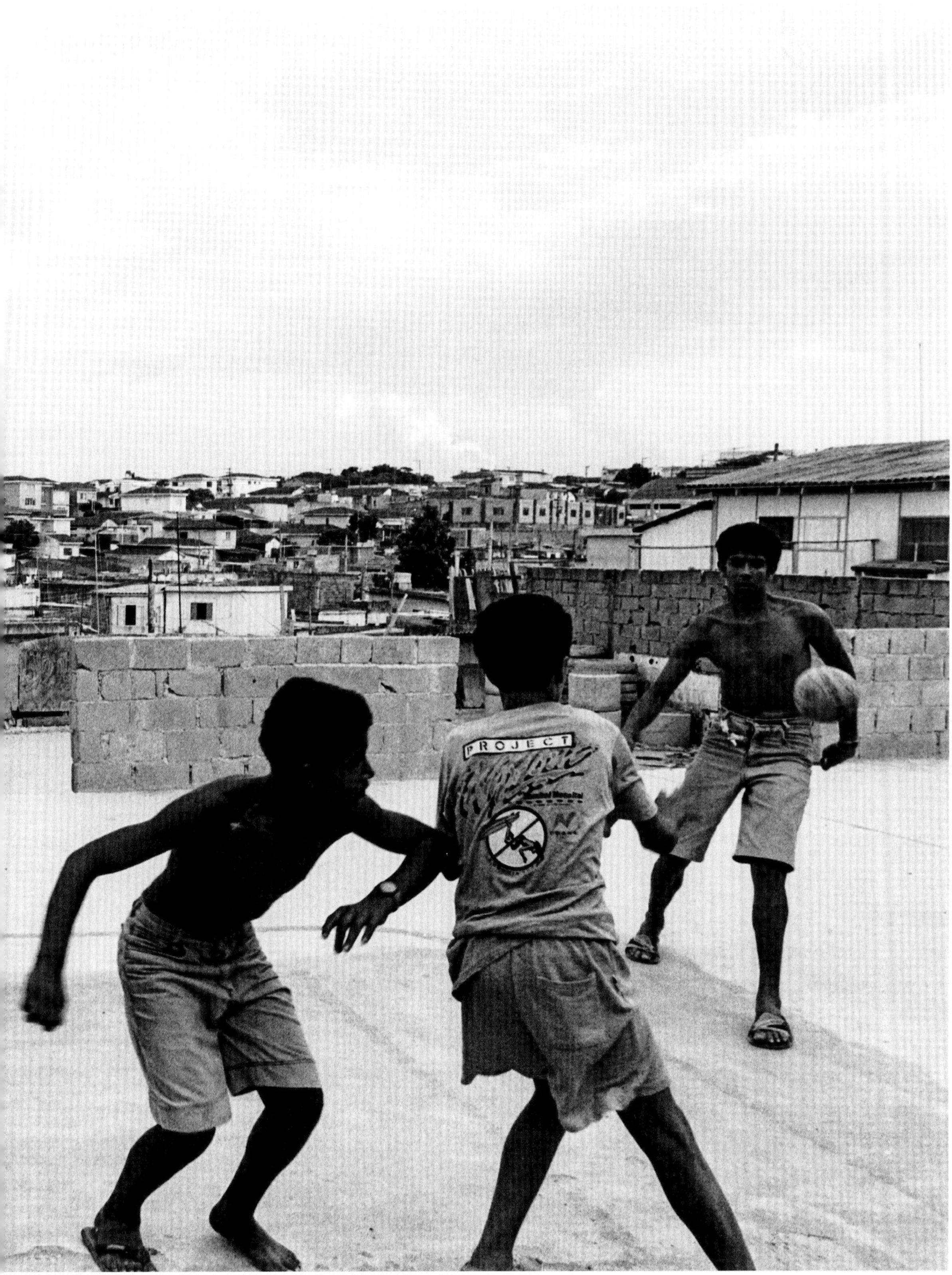
PROJECT

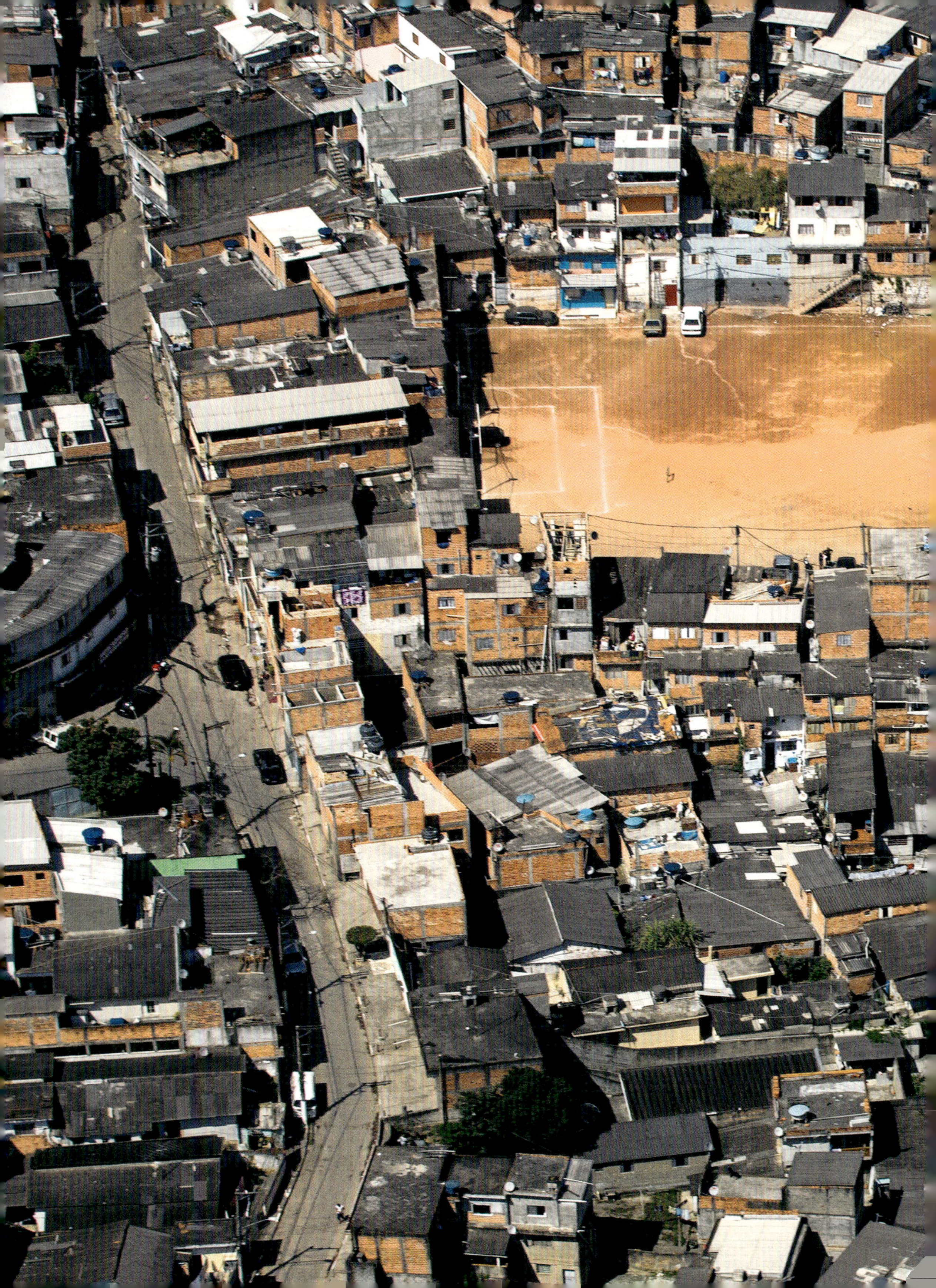

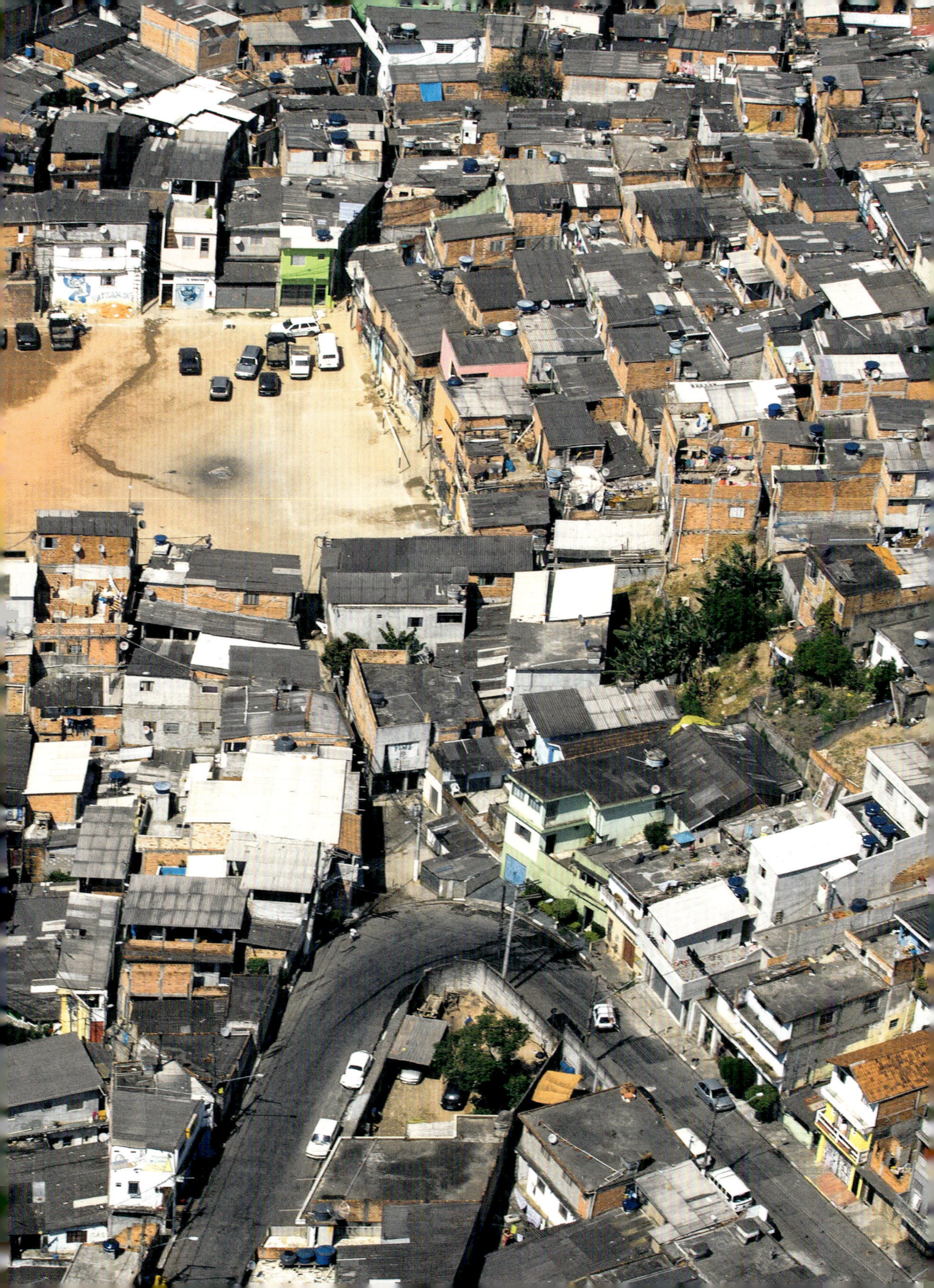

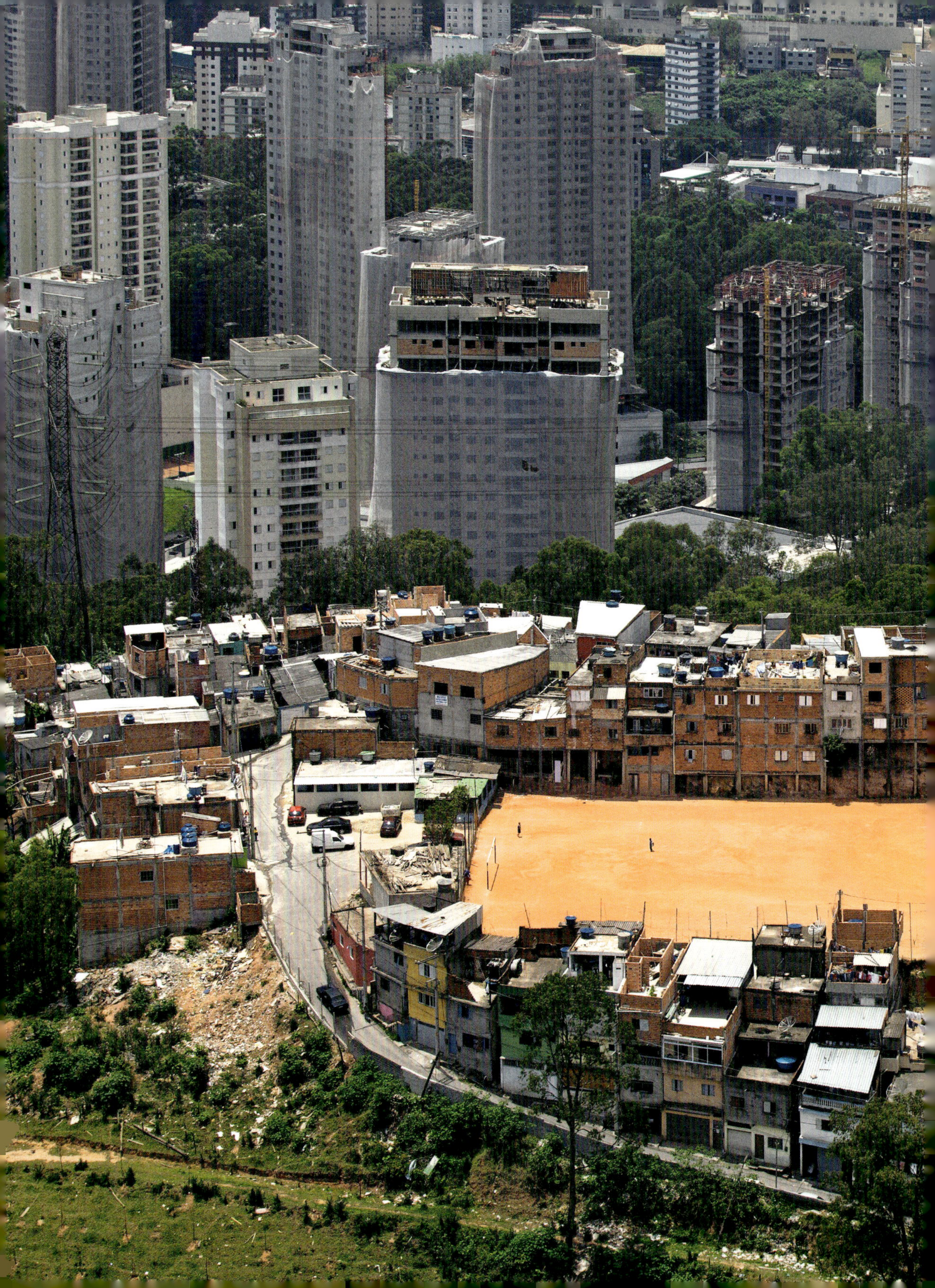

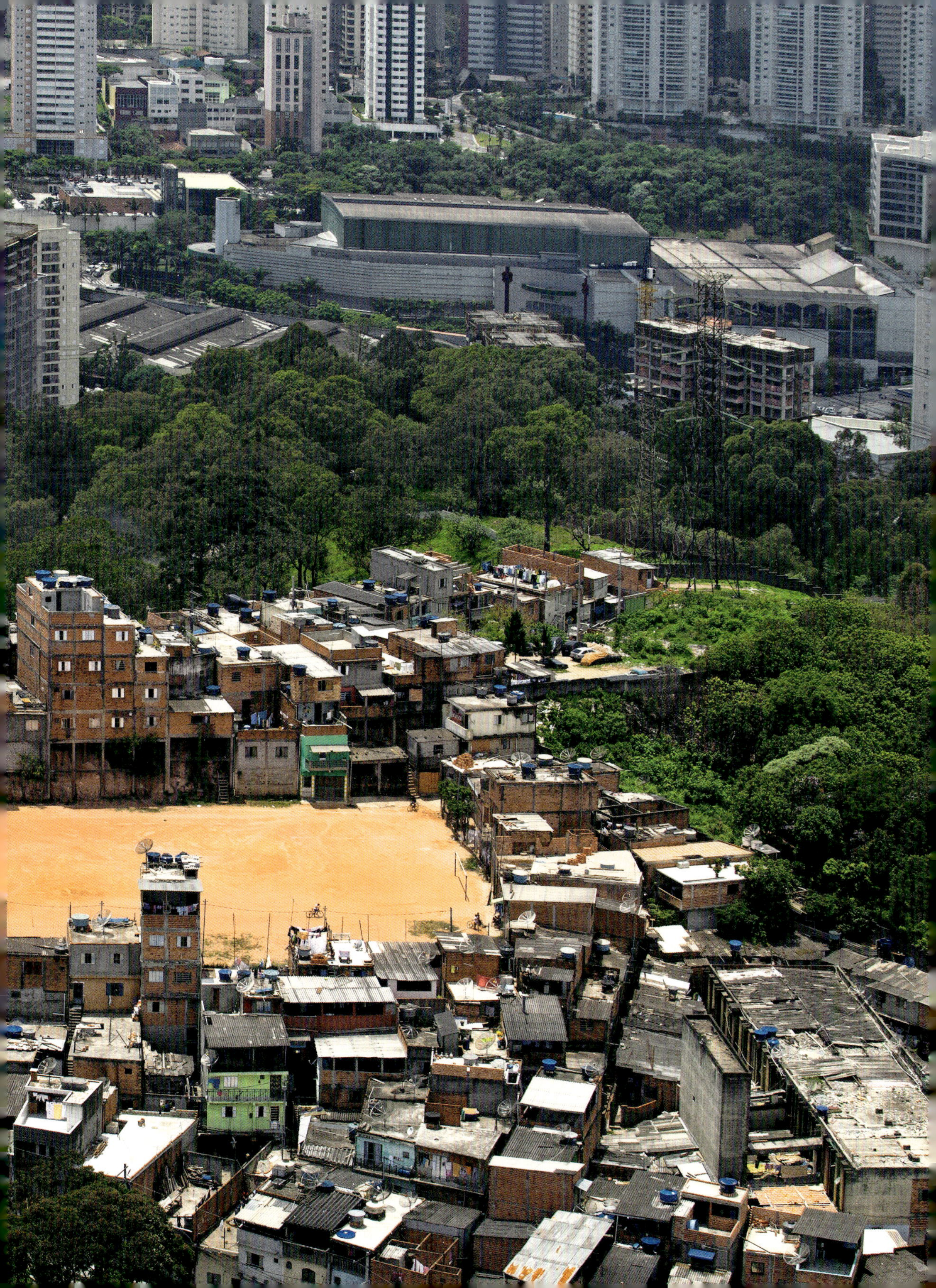

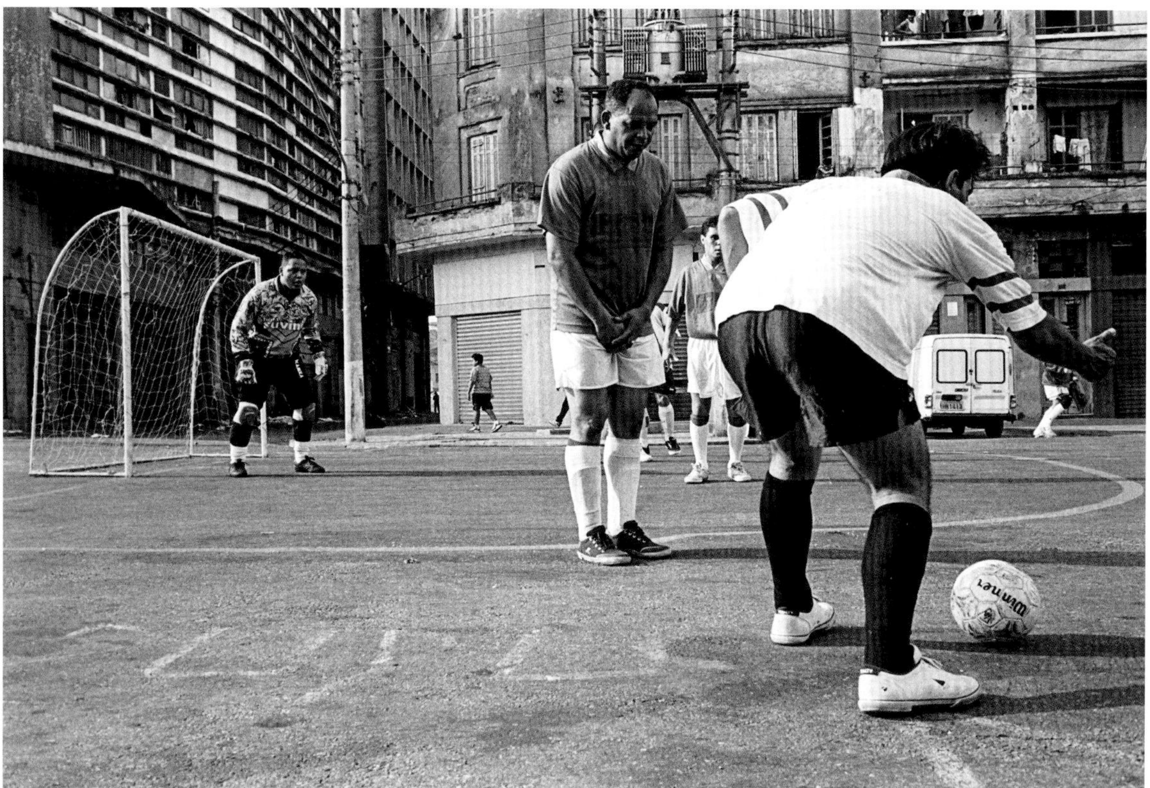

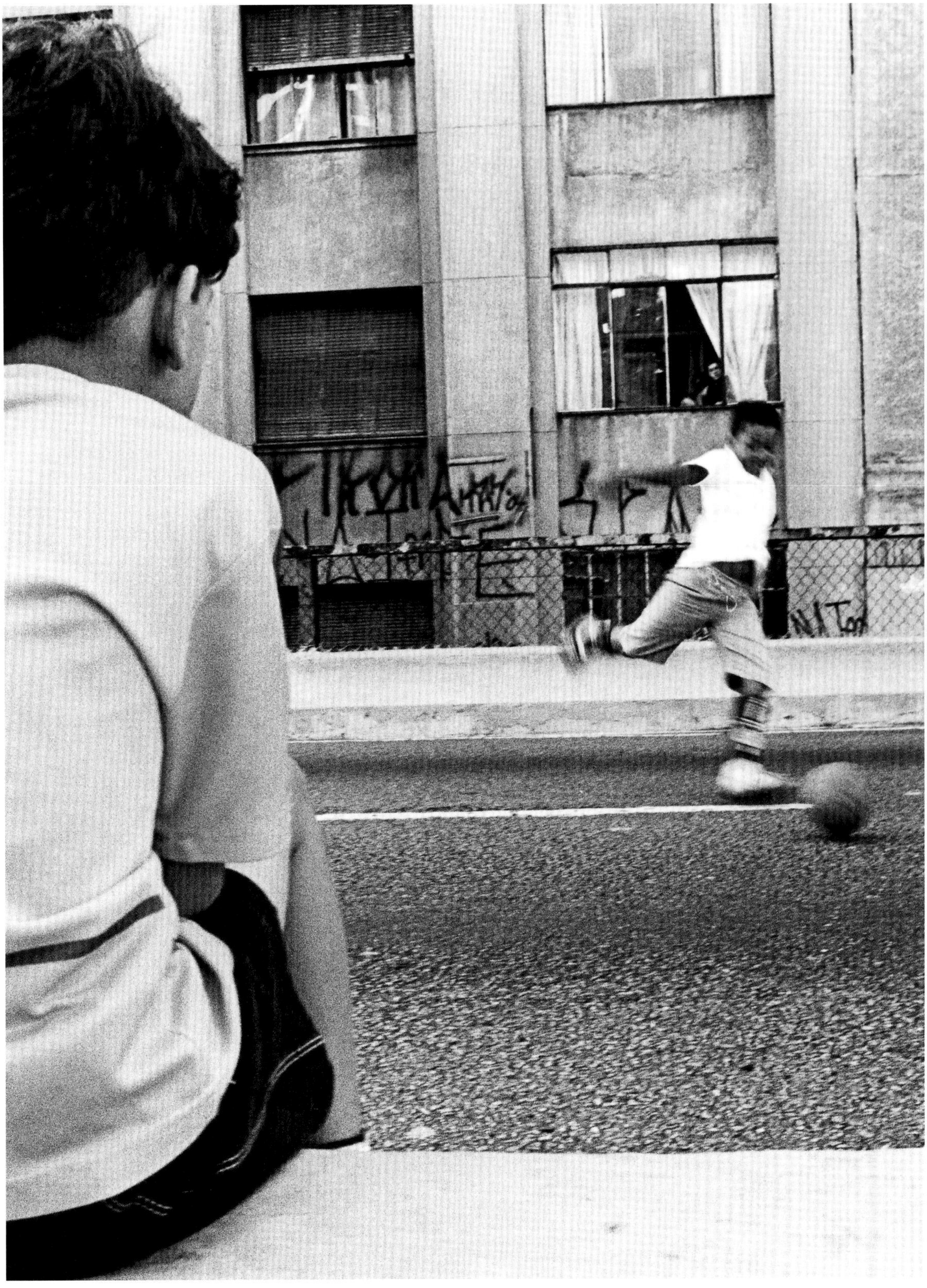

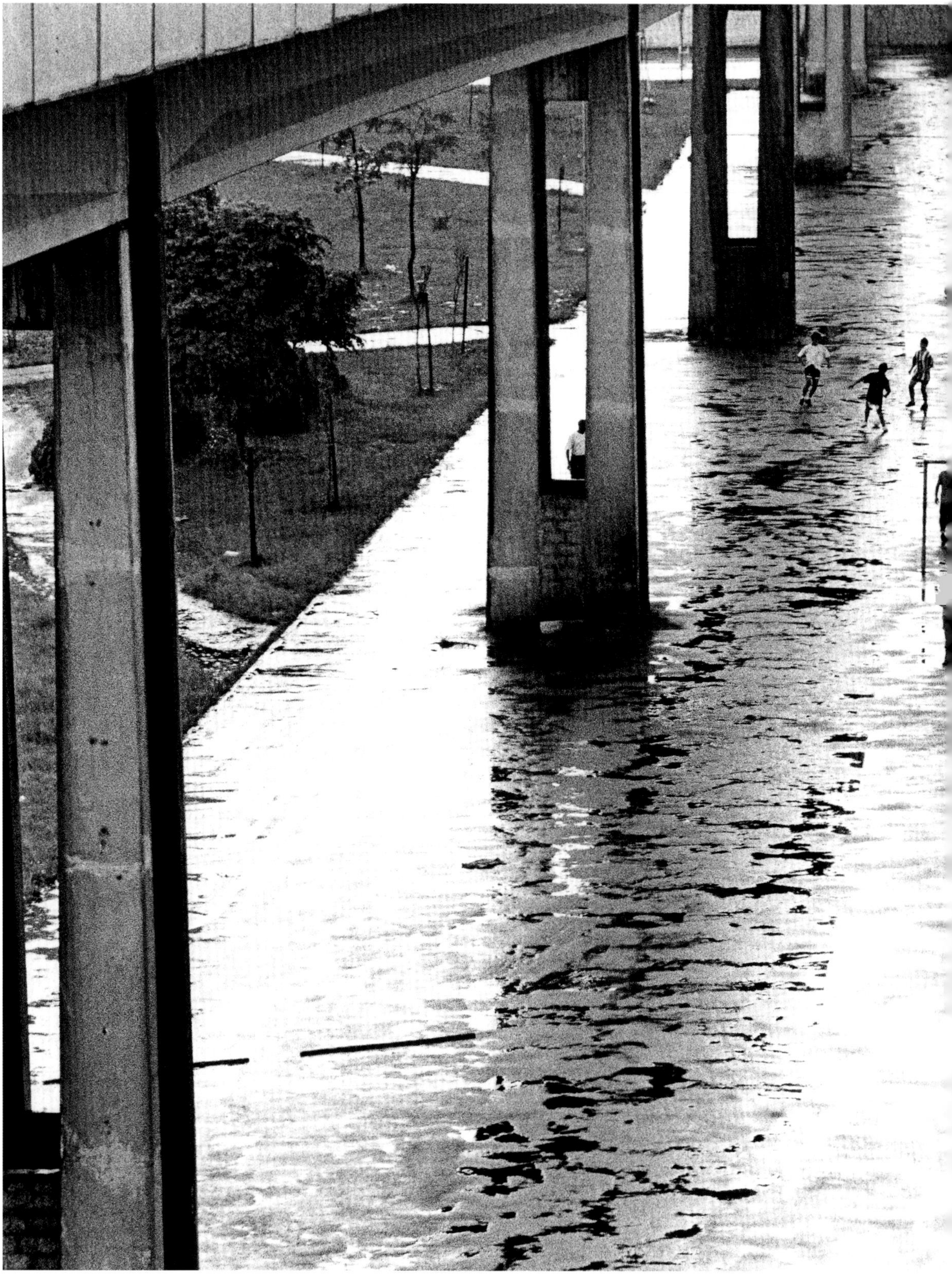

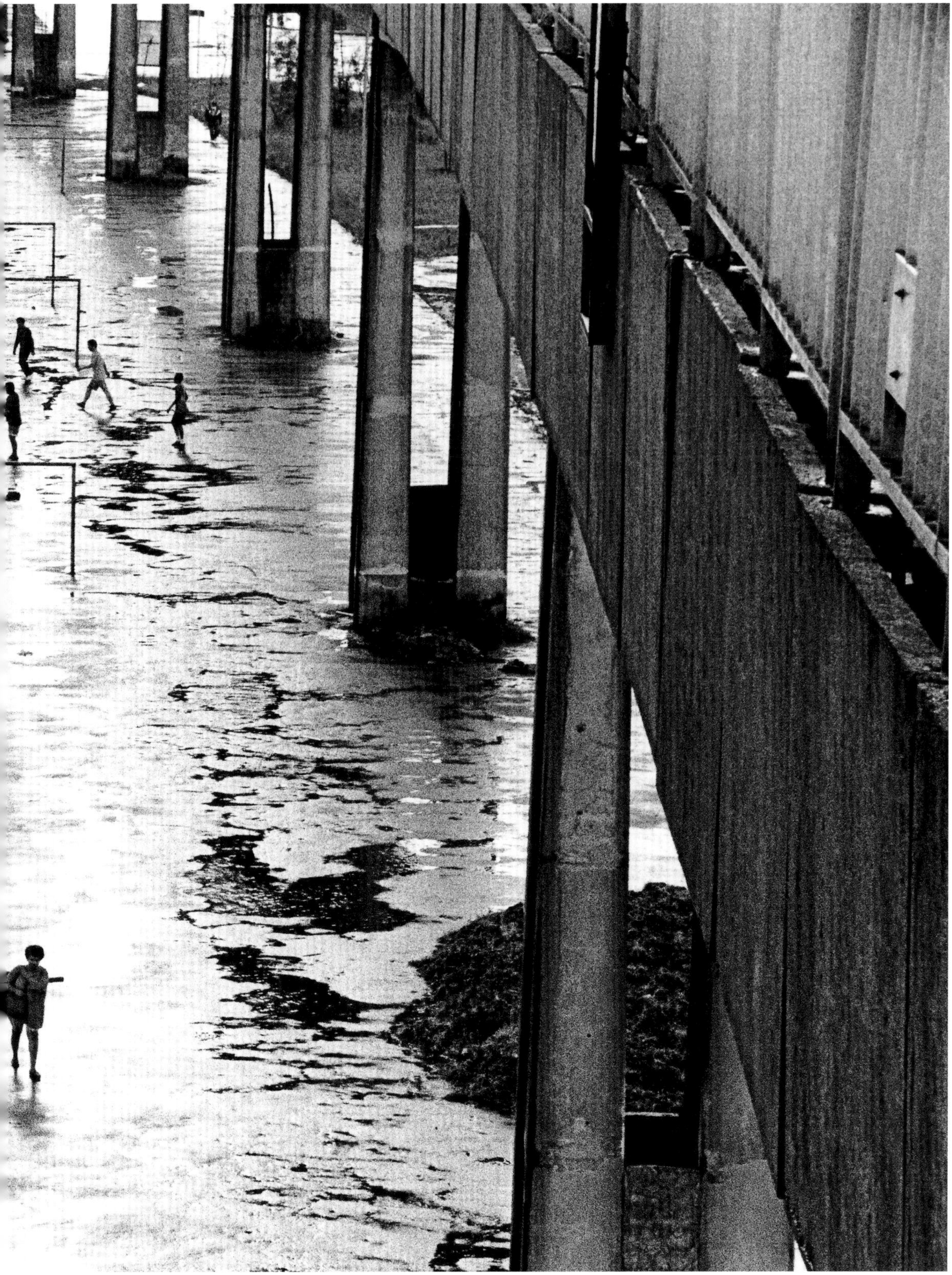

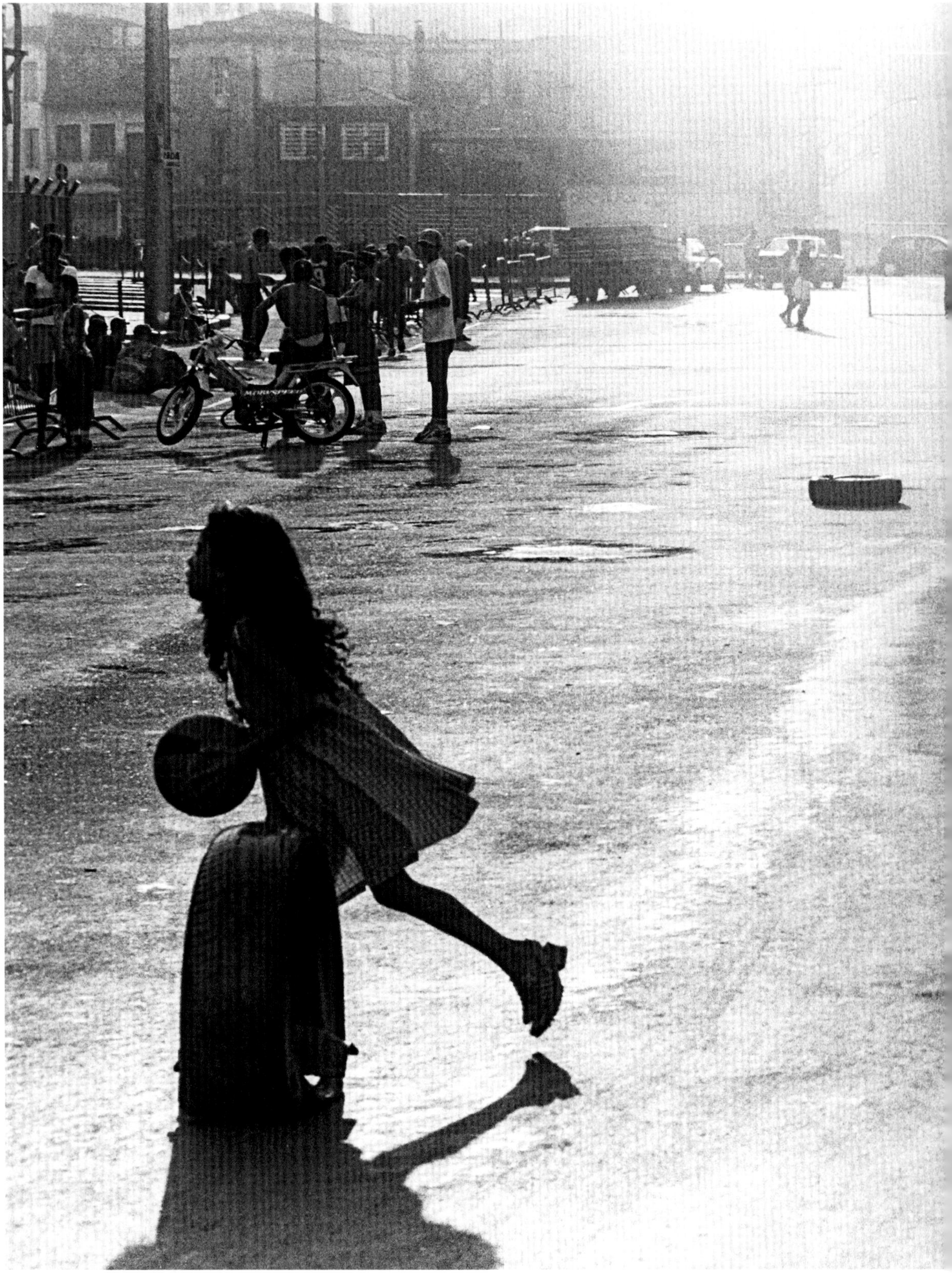

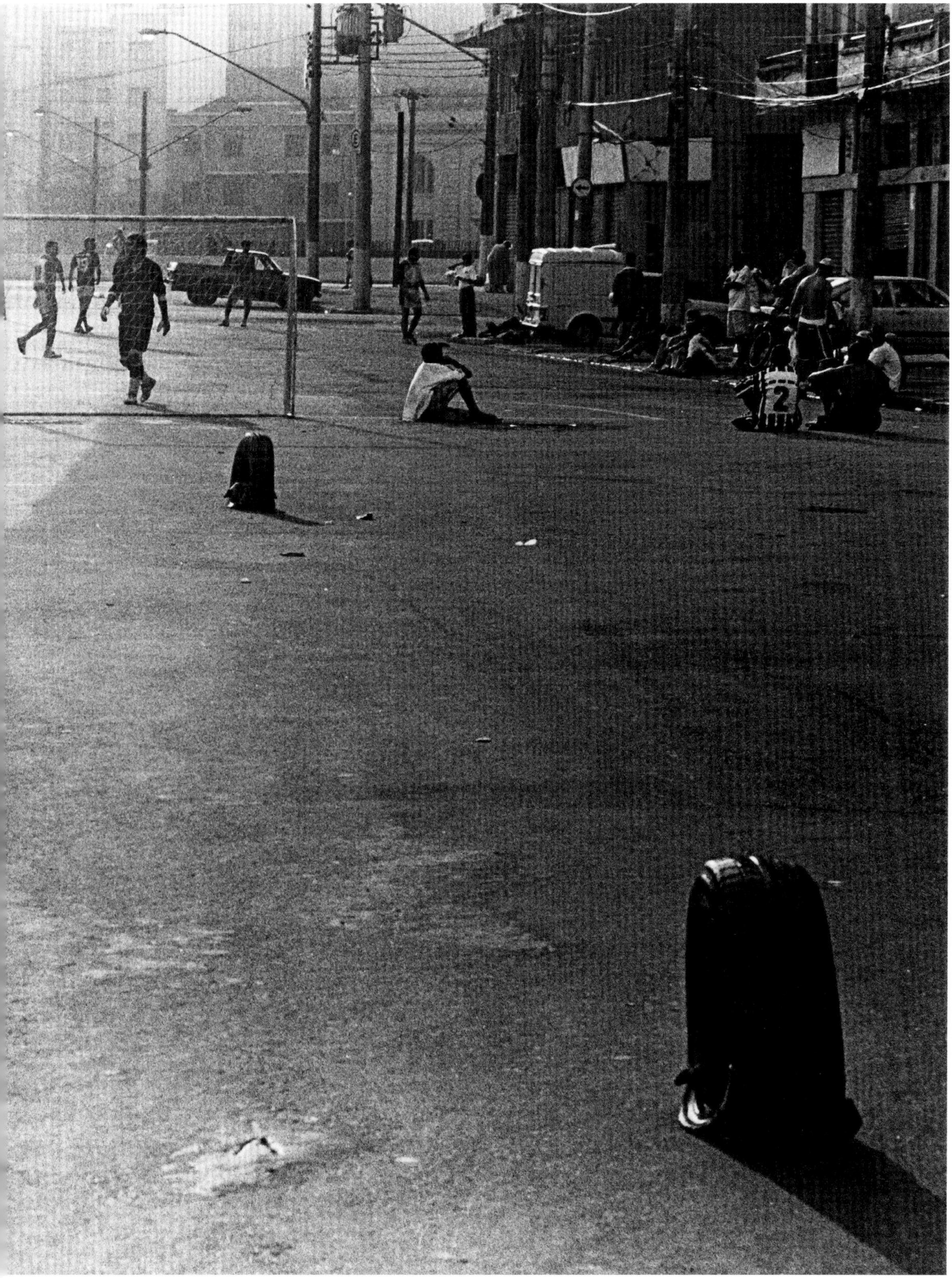

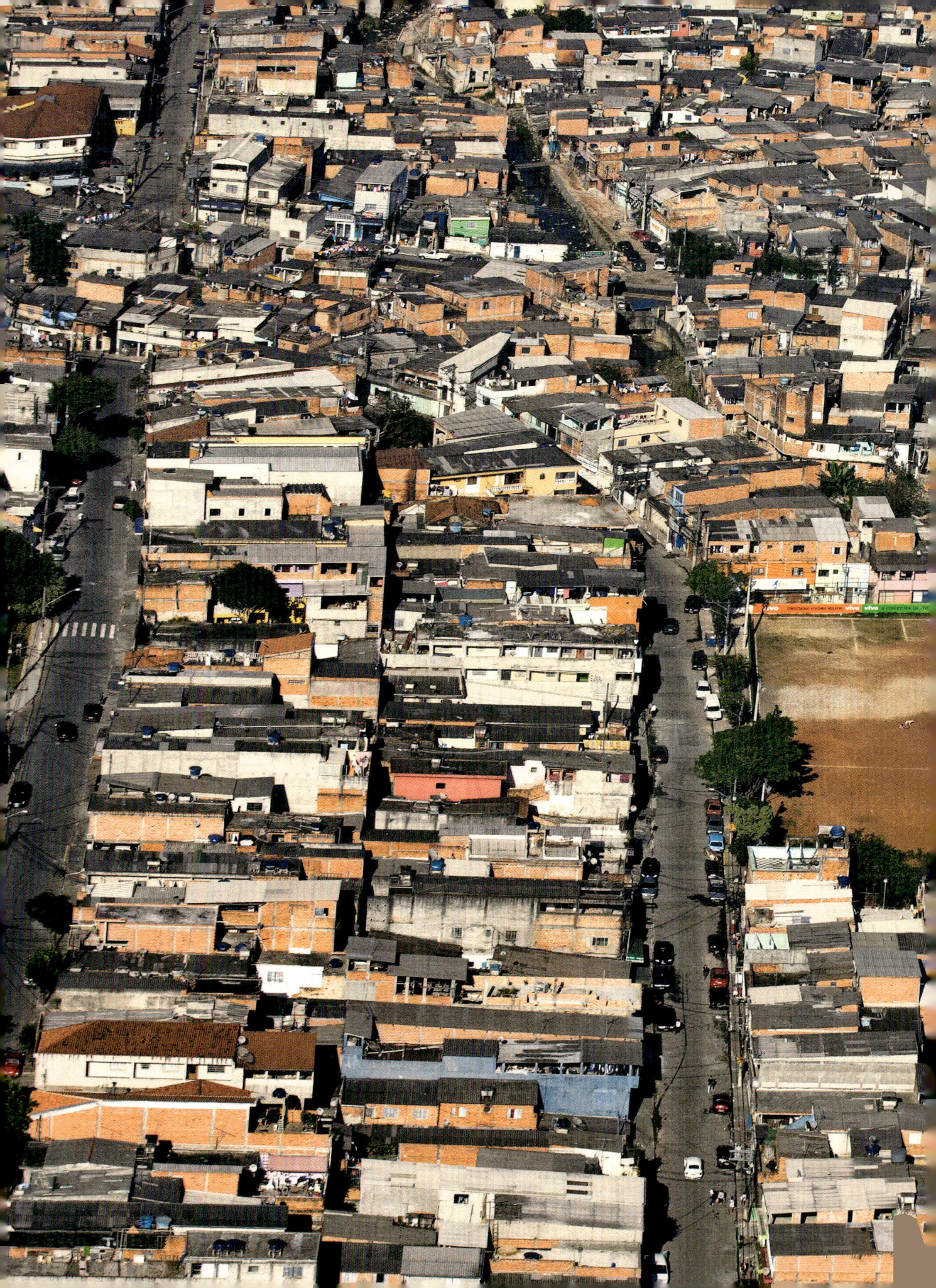

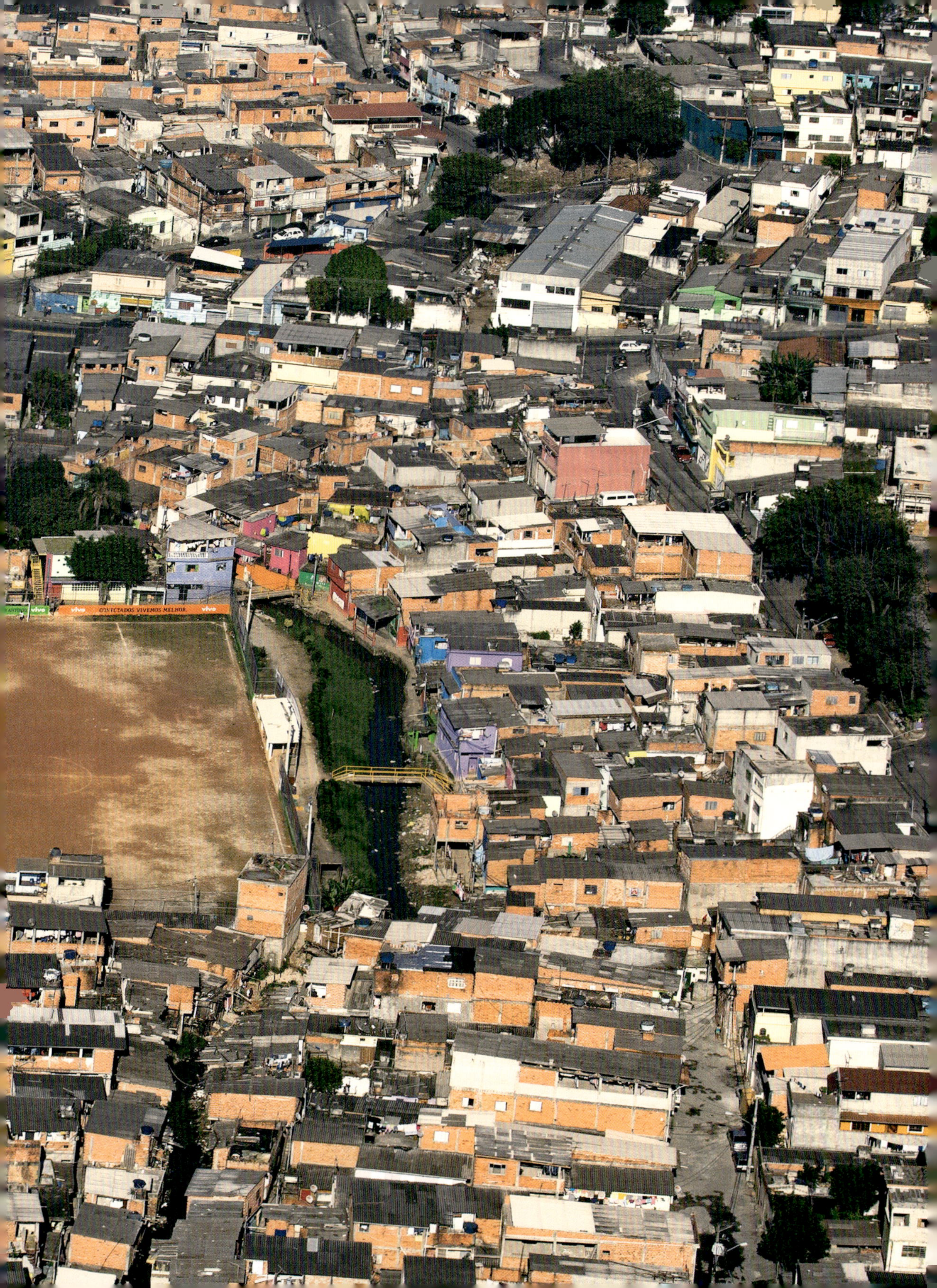
vivo
CONECTADOS VIVEMOS MELHOR.
vivo
vivo

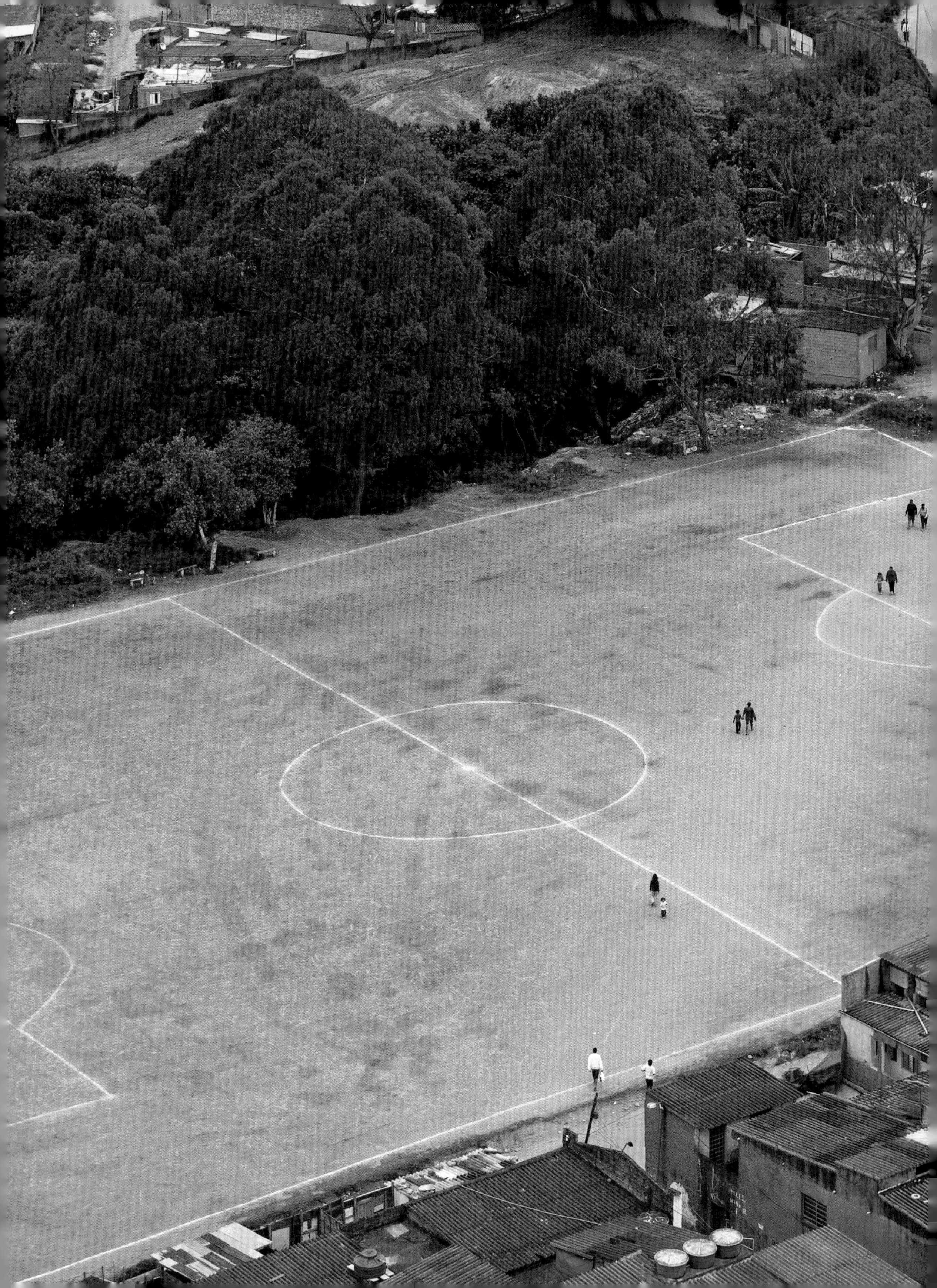

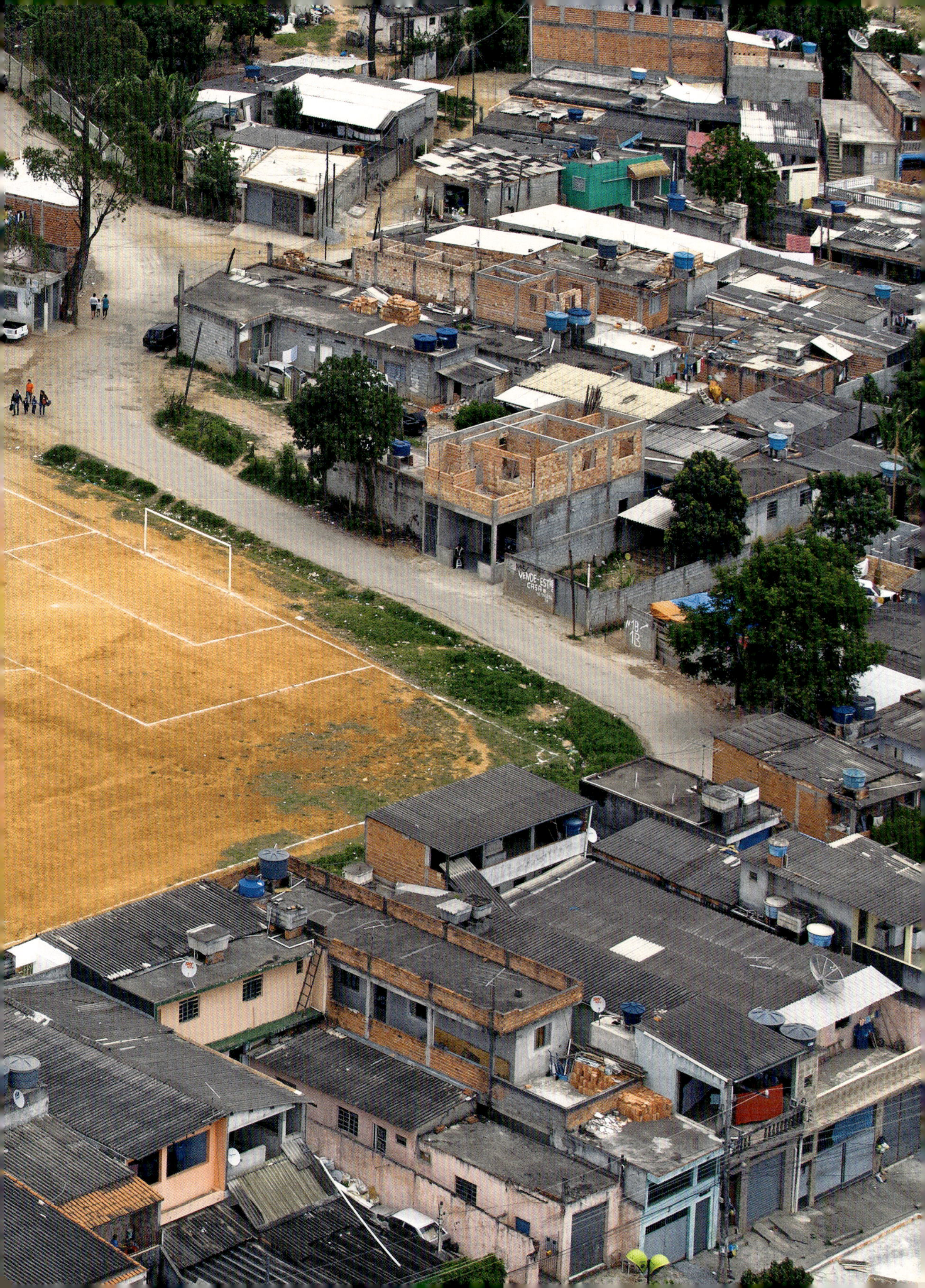
VENDE-ESTA
CASA

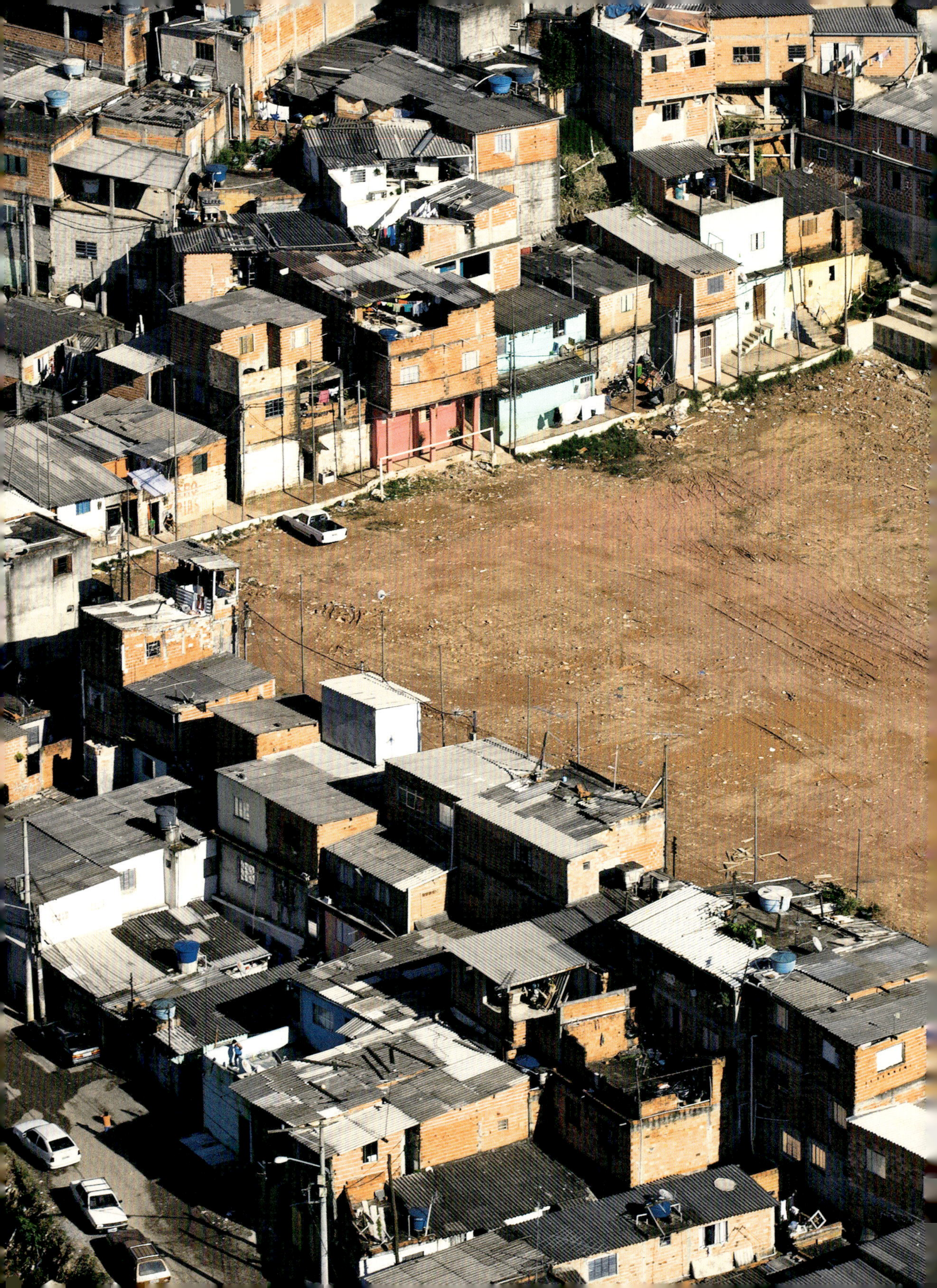

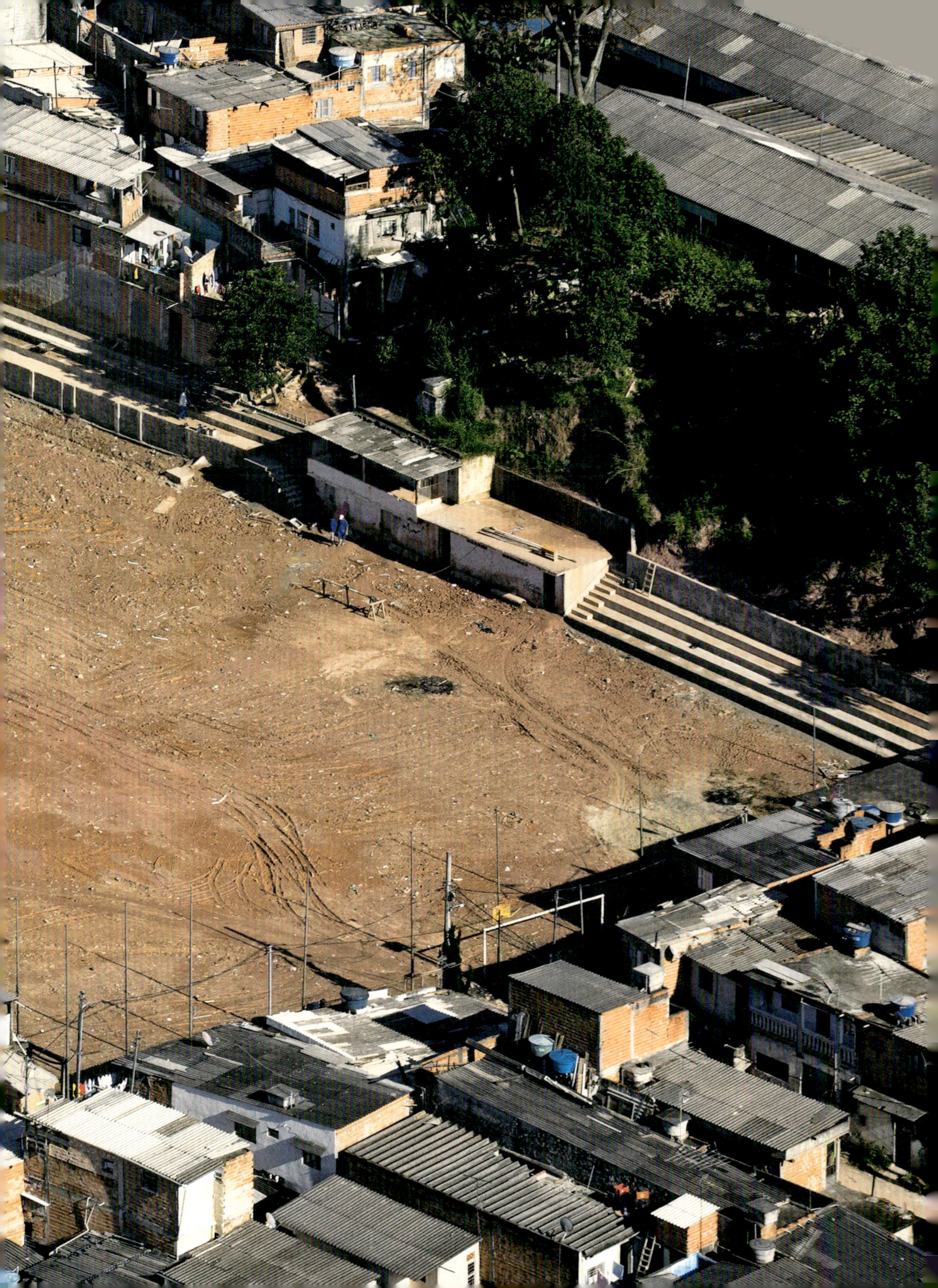

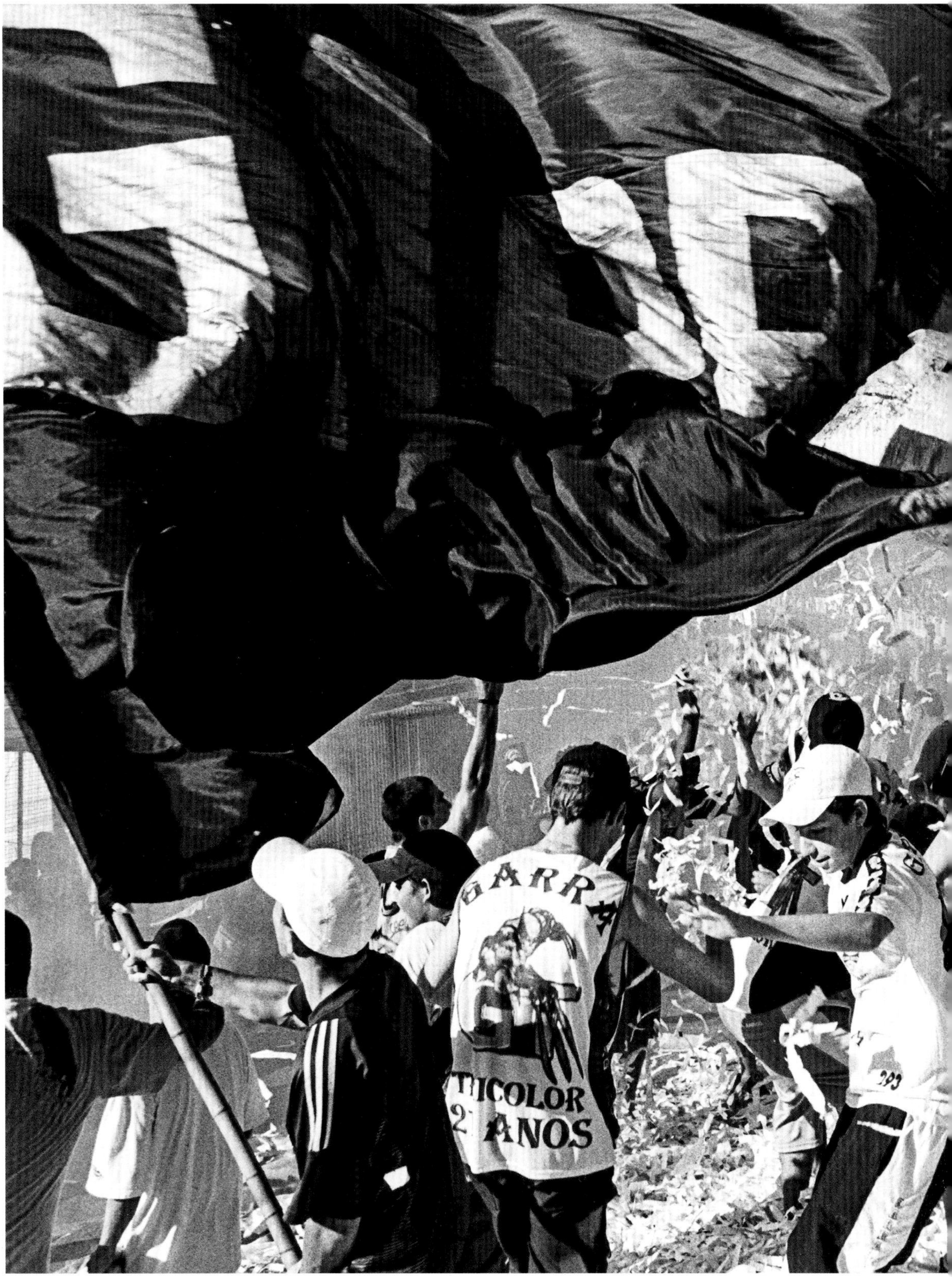
GARRA
TTICOLOR
ANOS

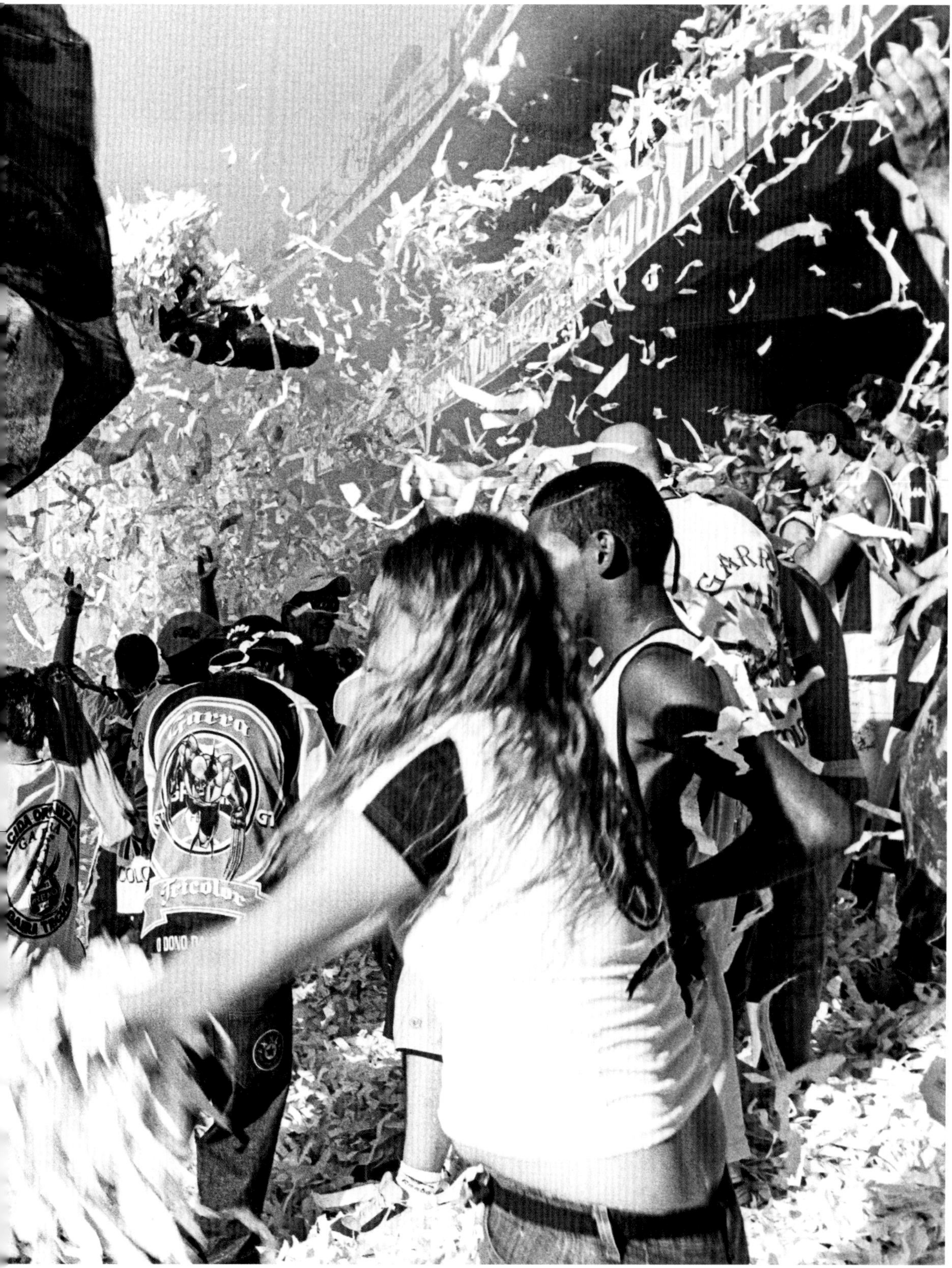
Garra
Tricolor

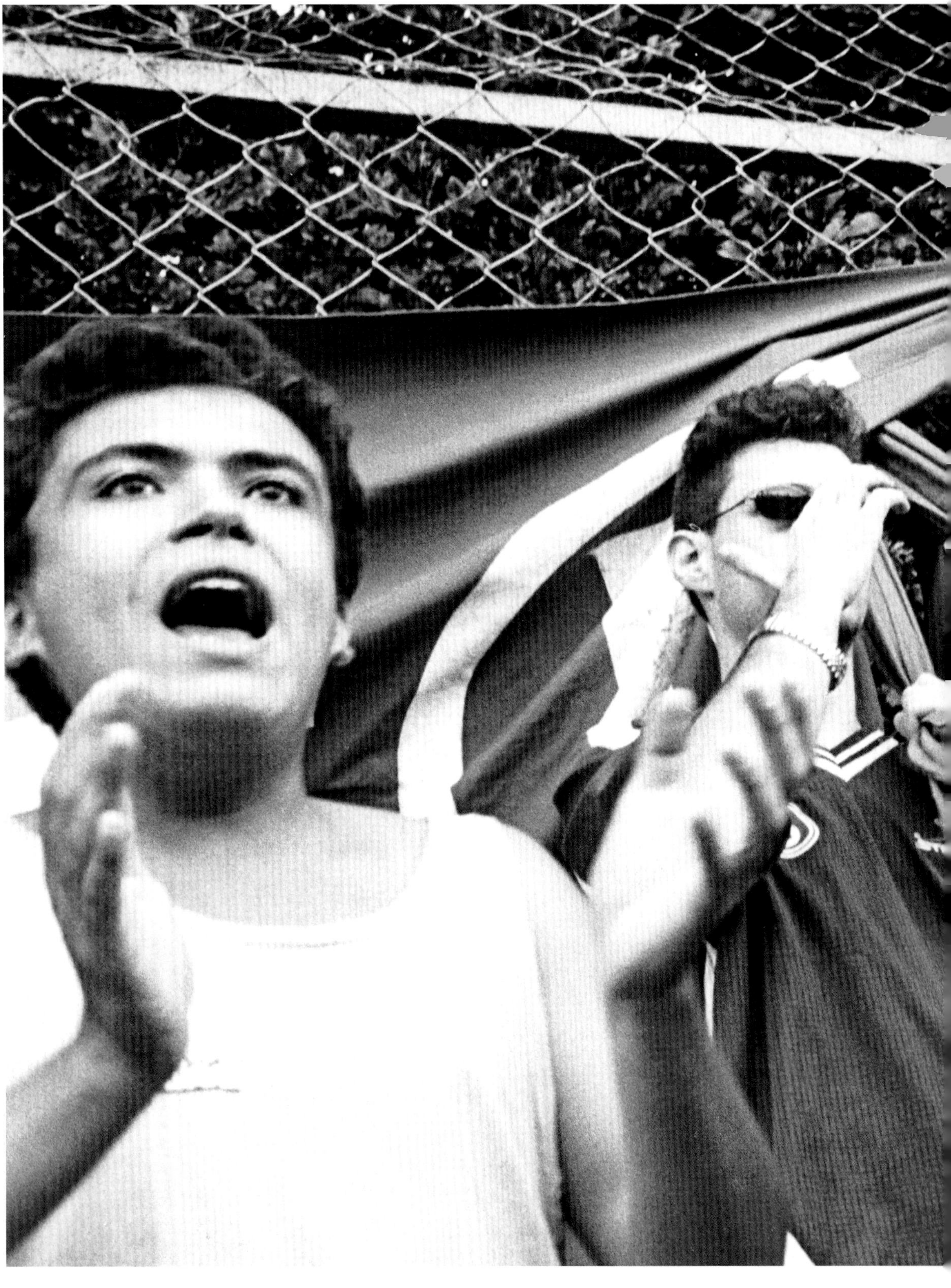

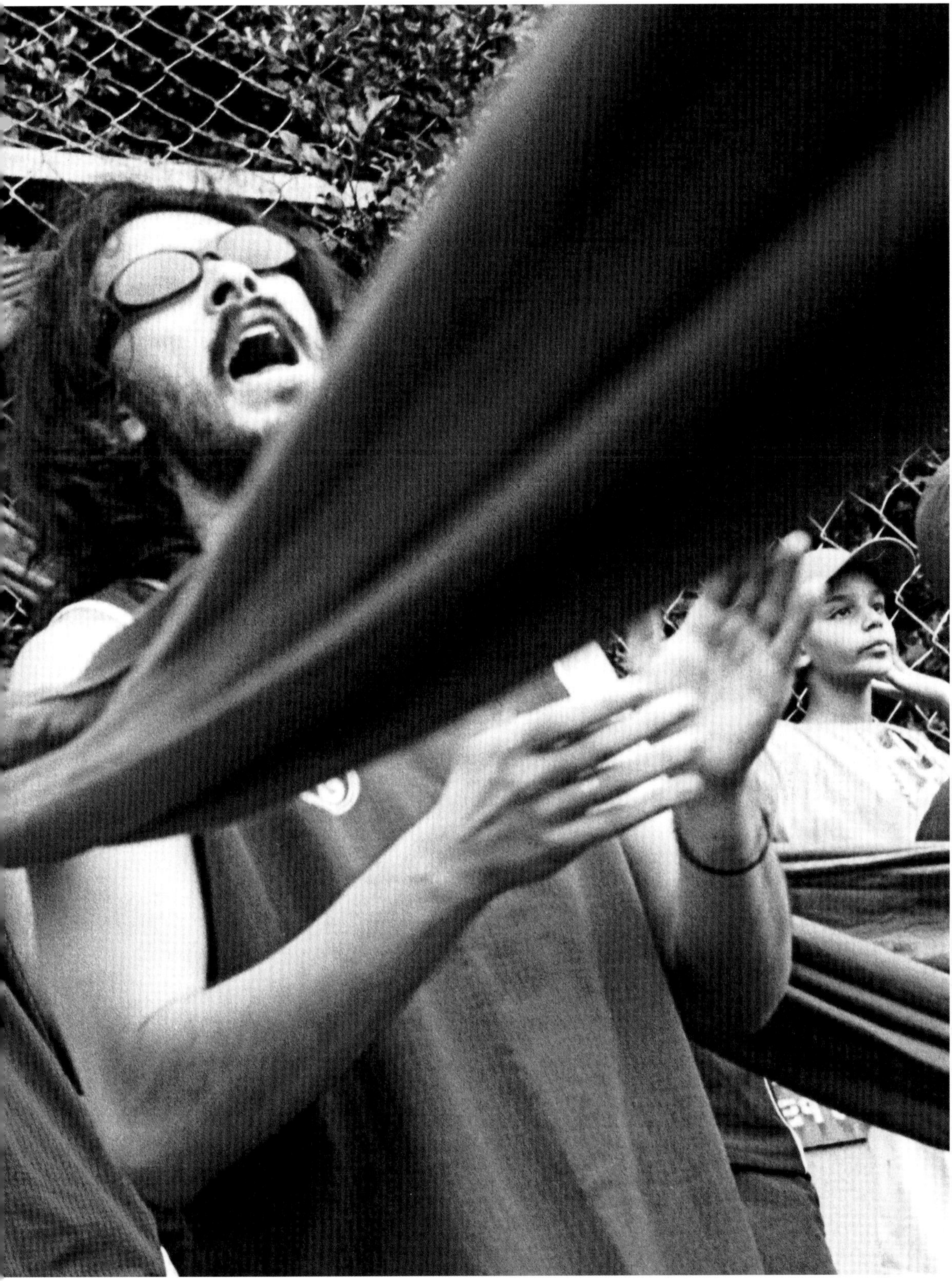

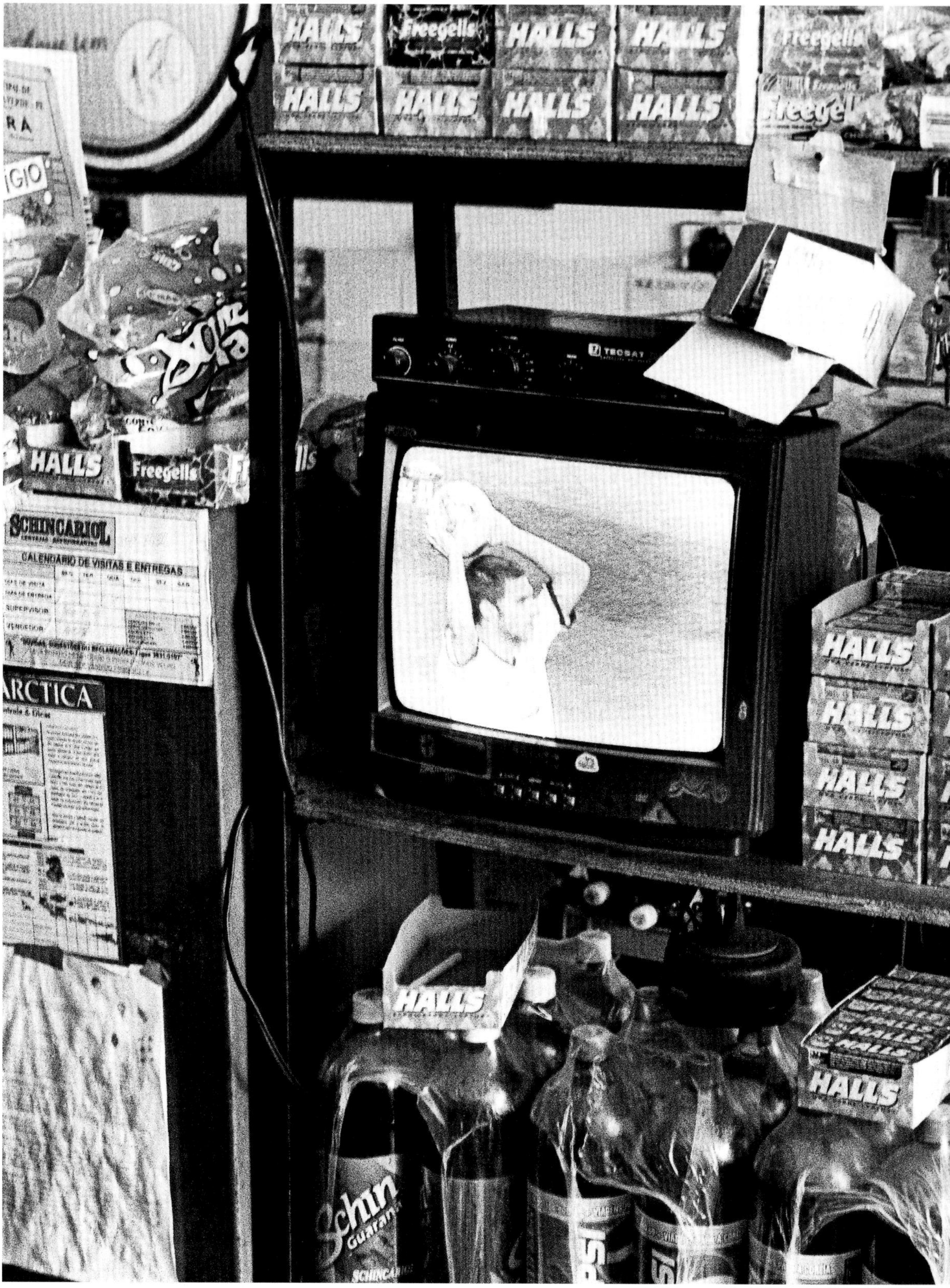
HALLS
Freegells
SCHINCARIOL
CALENDÁRIO DE VISITAS E ENTREGAS
ARCTICA
TECSAT

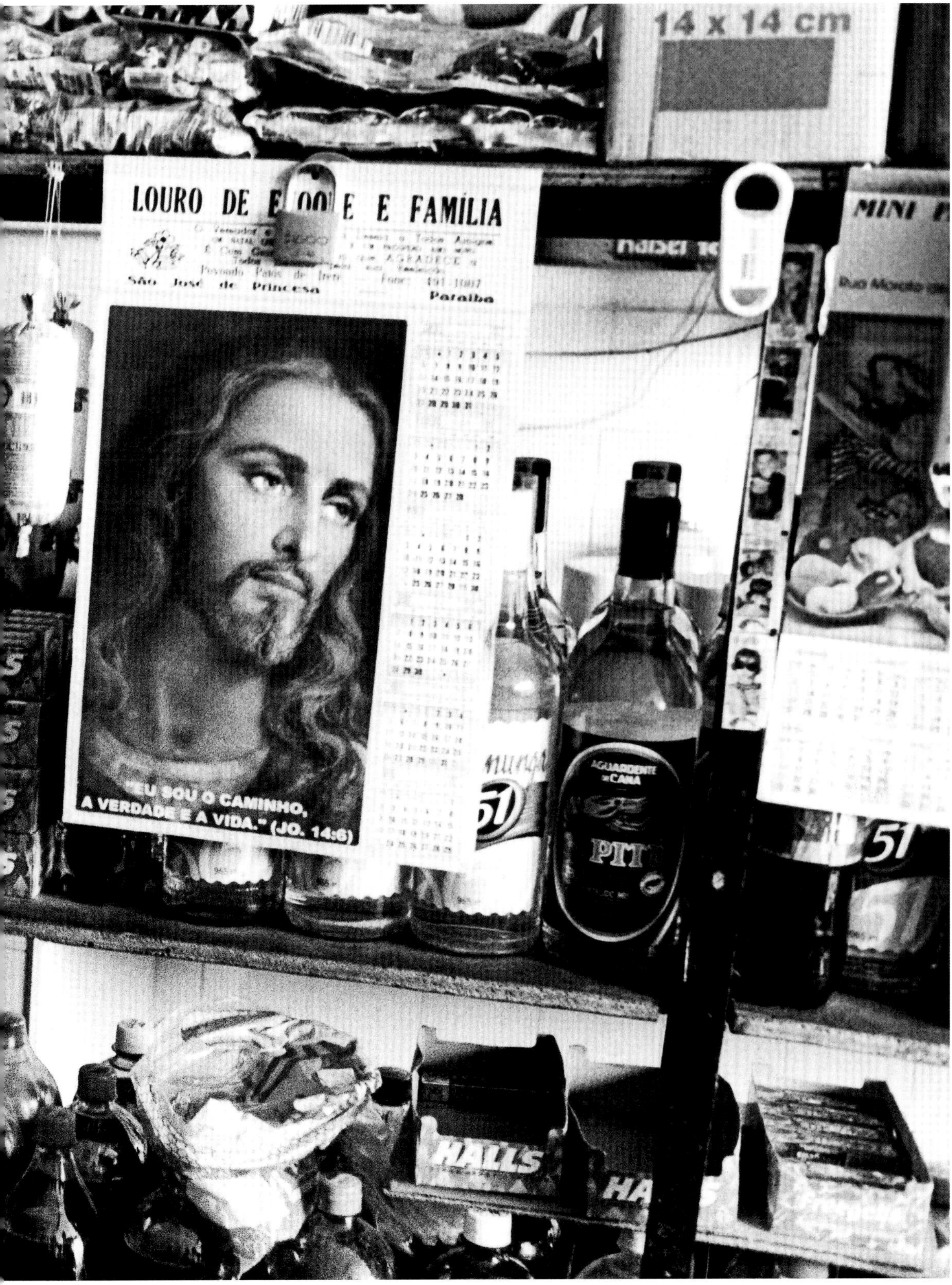
14 x 14 cm
São José de Princesa
Paraiba
"EU SOU O CAMINHO,
A VERDADE E A VIDA." (JO. 14:6)
AGUARDENTE DE CANA
HALLS

LEONARDO FINOTTI
born in 1977, is a Brazilian architectural photographer with an international reputation. Whether the results of commissions or his personal initiatives, his photos are published in leading specialist journals and publications all over the world. He also shows his work in solo and group exhibitions, and runs Obra Comunicação, a collaborative communication office that produces articles, exhibitions, and catalogues. As this present book shows, he is becoming increasingly involved in the art world.

Campos Sagrados is a sequence of aerial photographs taken by Leonardo Finotti from 2007 to 2013. The series is an inventory of improvised and proper soccer pitches on the periphery of São Paulo.

ED VIGGIANI
born in São Paulo in 1958, took up photography in 1978. At the beginning of the 1980s he worked with Chico Albuquerque at the daily newspaper *O Povo* in Fortaleza, and was also his assistant. He later worked for the magazine *IstoÉ*, the *Folha de S. Paulo* daily, and the *Jornal do Brasil*'s São Paulo edition. For his first solo exhibition, *Matando o Tempo a Golpe de Luz* (1991), at the Fotoptica Gallery, São Paulo, he received the Art Critics Association Award (APCA/SP) for the best exhibition of the year. Other awards include the U.S. Mother Jones International Fund for Documentary Photography (1991), for *Irmãos de Fé*, a photo-essay on popular religion in Brazil. He created the concept for the book *Brasil Bom de Bola* (1998) and was its editorial coordinator.

In his photo series Brasileiros Futebol Clube, Ed Viggiani accompanies his fellow countrymen everywhere where soccer is played or a team followed.

AFONSO CELSO GÁRCIA REIS
born in 1947 and best known as Afonsinho, is a Brazilian soccer legend. A rebel soul with a generous heart, in 1971, at the height of the military dictatorship, he became the first player under the regime to negotiate his own transfer to another club, decades before a similar system was adopted in Europe. Afonsinho has entered Brazilian popular culture as the subject both of a ballad written by the famous songwriter Gilberto Gil, and of the documentary film *Passe Livre* (1974) by Oswaldo Caldeira.

Today Afonso Celso Gárcia Reis works as a psychiatrist at Philippe Pinel Institute in Rio de Janeiro and writes a column on society and soccer for *Carta Capital,* a leading Brazilian magazine.

LUÍS ANTÔNIO JORGE
is an architect and urbanist who graduated from PUC Campinas (1985), and received his masters degree (1993) and Ph.D. (1999) in Architecture and Urbanism from the University of São Paulo (USP). He has had his own office since 1986, being a founding partner of the Casa da Arquitetura in Campinas. He currently devotes much of his time to teaching and research at the Faculty of Architecture and Urbanism, University of São Paulo (FAU/USP).

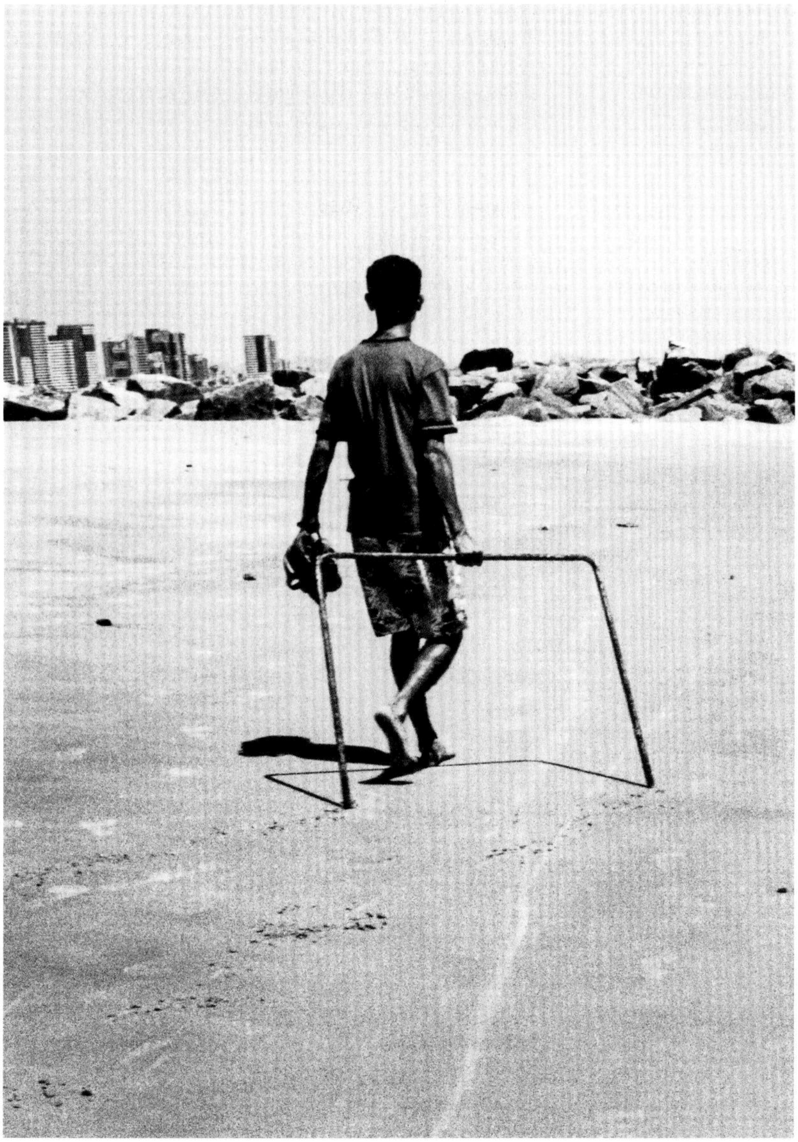

FUTEBOL
URBAN EUPHORIA IN BRAZIL

Edited by Lars Müller
Concept: Lars Müller and Leonardo Finotti
Photography: Leonardo Finotti, Ed Viggiani
Design: Integral Lars Müller / Lars Müller and Natascha Kuhn
Coordintaion: Lars Müller Publishers / Rebekka Kiesewetter
Copyediting / Proofreading: Chris Murray
Translations: Elizabeth Lowe McCoy (BP-E)

Lithography: Ast & Fischer, Wabern
Printing and binding: Kösel, Altusried-Krugzell, Germany
Paper: LuxoArt Samt, 150 g/m²

Lars Müller Publishers
Zürich, Switzerland
www.lars-mueller-publishers.com

ISBN 978-3-03778-431-0

Printed in Germany

DON BOSCO
Jugendhilfe Weltweit
www.donbosco.ch

Lars Müller Publishers supports the Swiss youth relief agency Don Bosco Jugendhilfe Weltweit and donates parts of the revenues from their sales to the campaign Bosco Arena.

The campaign Bosco Arena shows how the Salesians of Don Bosco keep children and young people off the streets with the aid of soccer and how they support and encourage them to attend a school and to learn a profession. The campaign concretely assists two projects which are supported by Don Bosco Jugendhilfe Weltweit: The only school of the Favela Jacarezinho in Rio de Janeiro, where 100,000 people live on one square kilometer, and the charitable organization Don Bosco with the vocational training center in the Itaquera district of São Paulo, where 1,700 young women and men receive an education with professional qualifications.